10759472
A Time
FOR
Everything
52-Week
Devotional
Journal
for Women
BELLE
CITY
GIFTS

Belle City Gifts
Savage, Minnesota, USA
Belle City Gifts is an imprint of BroadStreet Publishing Group, LLC.
Broadstreetpublishing.com

A Time for Everything

9781424568895

Typesetting and design by Garborg Design Works | garborgdesign.com

Compiled and edited by Michelle Winger | literallyprecise.com

Printed in China.

24 25 26 27 28 29 30 7 6 5 4 3 2 1

There is a time for everything,
and everything on earth
has its special season.

ECCLESIASTES 3:1 NCV

Introduction

This beautifully designed devotional journal for women features meditations, thought-provoking prompts and questions, and encouraging quotes and Scriptures that will help your weekly devotional life to be focused and intentional.

There is a time for everything, and this moment is yours to reflect and consider. Pray with a heart full of gratitude and hope, confident that the Father is ever near, listening with a tender heart of compassion.

Reflect on the promises of God, delight in his goodness, and express your thoughts, prayers, and praise in the space provided.

WEEK 1

All Things

> He has made everything beautiful in its time.
> He has also set eternity in the human heart;
> yet no one can fathom what God has done
> from beginning to end.
>
> ECCLESIASTES 3:11 NIV

We've probably all heard an older gentleman declare that his wife is more beautiful now than the day they married. And we likely thought, *He needs glasses.* What we fail to recognize in our outward-focused, airbrushed society, is that time really does make things beautiful. More accurately, time gives us a better perspective on the true definition of beauty. Spending time with those we love affords us a glimpse into the depth of beauty that lies within. So while the external beauty may be fading, there is a wealth of beauty inside.

God's Word says that he makes all things beautiful in his time. *All* things. Whatever situation you are facing right now has the potential to create beauty in you. Perseverance, humility, grace, obedience—these are beautiful. But there's more. The beauty God creates in you cannot be fully described in human terms! There is eternal beauty to be found.

When you are met with challenges, run to your Father and sit in his presence. When you dwell there, you reflect his character. Allow the difficulties in your life to become a catalyst for true beauty.

Reflection

What is creating true beauty in you during this season?

MY THOUGHTS

MY RESPONSE

God's riches are very great, and his wisdom and knowledge have no end! No one can explain the things God decides or understand his ways.

ROMANS 11:33 NCV

To me, this Scripture feels most like (check one)

☐ A PROMISE ☐ AN INSTRUCTION ☐ A TRUTH

Here's how it impacts me...

Prayer

GRATITUDE

REQUESTS

WEEK 2

Moment of Solitude

In the morning, having risen a long while before daylight, He went out and departed to a solitary place; and there He prayed.

MARK 1:35 NKJV

When do you find time to pray? Even if we are intentional and passionate about prayer, the everyday activities in our life will almost always take priority over time with God. It is often said that prayer can happen at any time, and of course it does, but is there value in setting aside a specific time to communicate with God?

Did you ever realize that the notion of quiet times comes from the example set by Jesus? He would get up before daylight and pray in a solitary place. We are not often told what Jesus prayed about. It's not the content that matters; it's the willingness to maintain our relationship with the Father and seek his will.

Does this sound like you as you try to step away from the busyness of the day? Are people looking for you, pressing in on your alone time? Instead of trying to fit prayer into your busy day, pray before it gets busy, so you can cope with the pressures of life. Fight for your time with God. Be like Jesus and find time to wait on the Father.

How will you fit prayer time into your schedule?

MY THOUGHTS

MY RESPONSE

*At that time Jesus went off
to a mountain to pray,
and he spent the night praying to God.*

LUKE 6:12 NCV

To me, this Scripture feels most like (check one)

☐ A PROMISE ☐ AN INSTRUCTION ☐ A TRUTH

Here's how it impacts me...

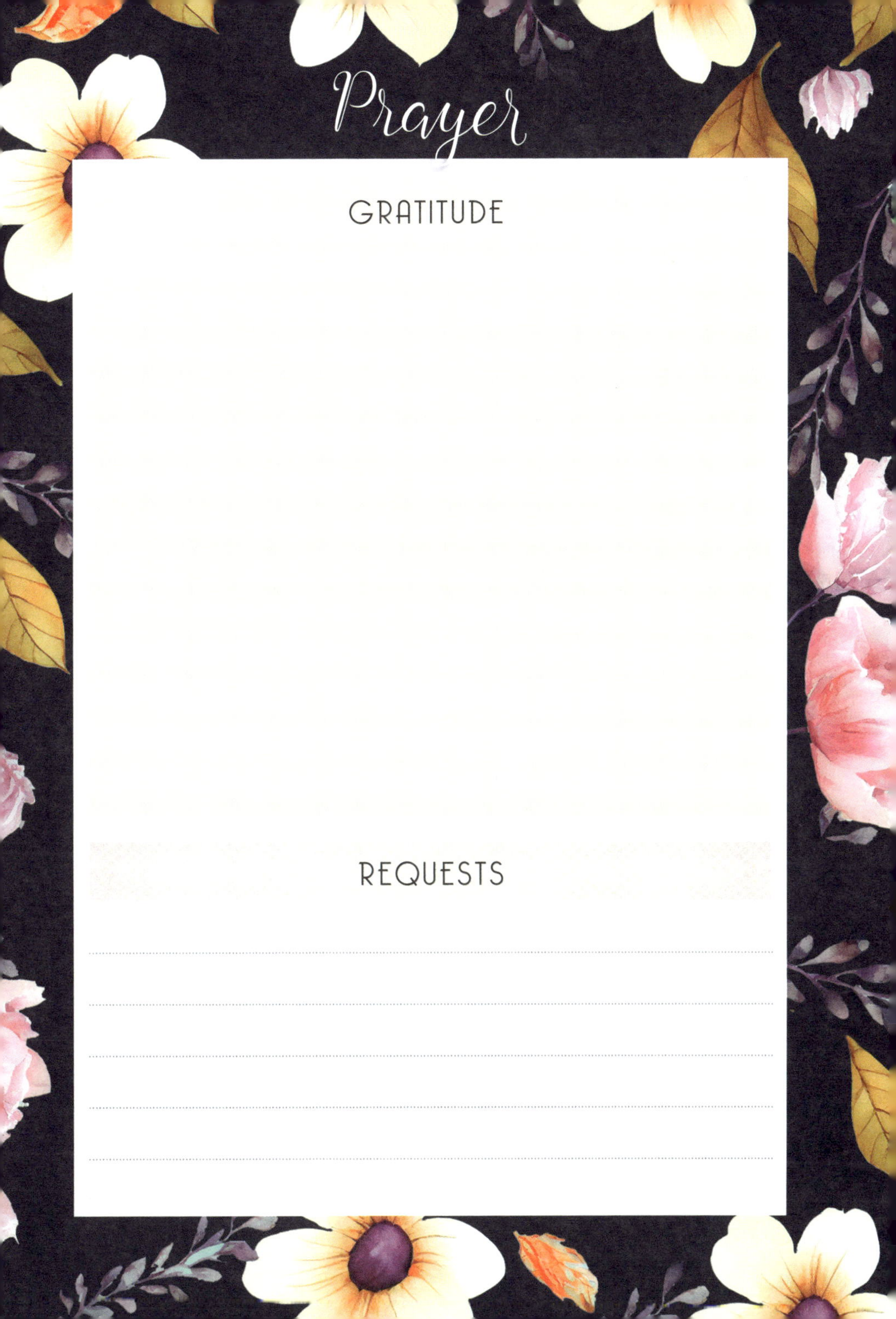
Prayer
GRATITUDE
REQUESTS

WEEK 3

One Step

> To him who is able to keep you from stumbling and to present you blameless before the presence of his glory with great joy, to the only God, our Savior, through Jesus Christ our Lord, be glory, majesty, dominion, and authority.
>
> JUDE 24-25 ESV

This race called *life* is a tiring one; sometimes the road gets long, and our legs threaten to buckle underneath heavy burdens. How do we persevere? Hear this glorious news: God, whose majesty is matchless, is waiting to hold you up under the weight you are carrying. He lifts the burden to his own strong shoulders. He keeps you from slipping and falling away. He brings you into his presence!

When the cold rains of sorrow or the sharp winds of discouragement are at our backs, press on and finish the race knowing that he is running with you. He is before you and behind you and beside you.

Run your race listening to the encouragement of your heavenly Father: his mighty shouts of everlasting joy! Take it one step at a time. Keep your eyes on him, and you will finish victoriously.

Reflection

Listen for God's encouraging voice as you take one step at a time. What do you hear him saying to you?

MY THOUGHTS

MY RESPONSE

The Lord will deliver me from every evil attack and will bring me safely into his heavenly Kingdom. All glory to God forever and ever! Amen.

2 TIMOTHY 4:18 NLT

To me, this Scripture feels most like (check one)

☐ A PROMISE ☐ AN INSTRUCTION ☐ A TRUTH

Here's how it impacts me...

Prayer

GRATITUDE

REQUESTS

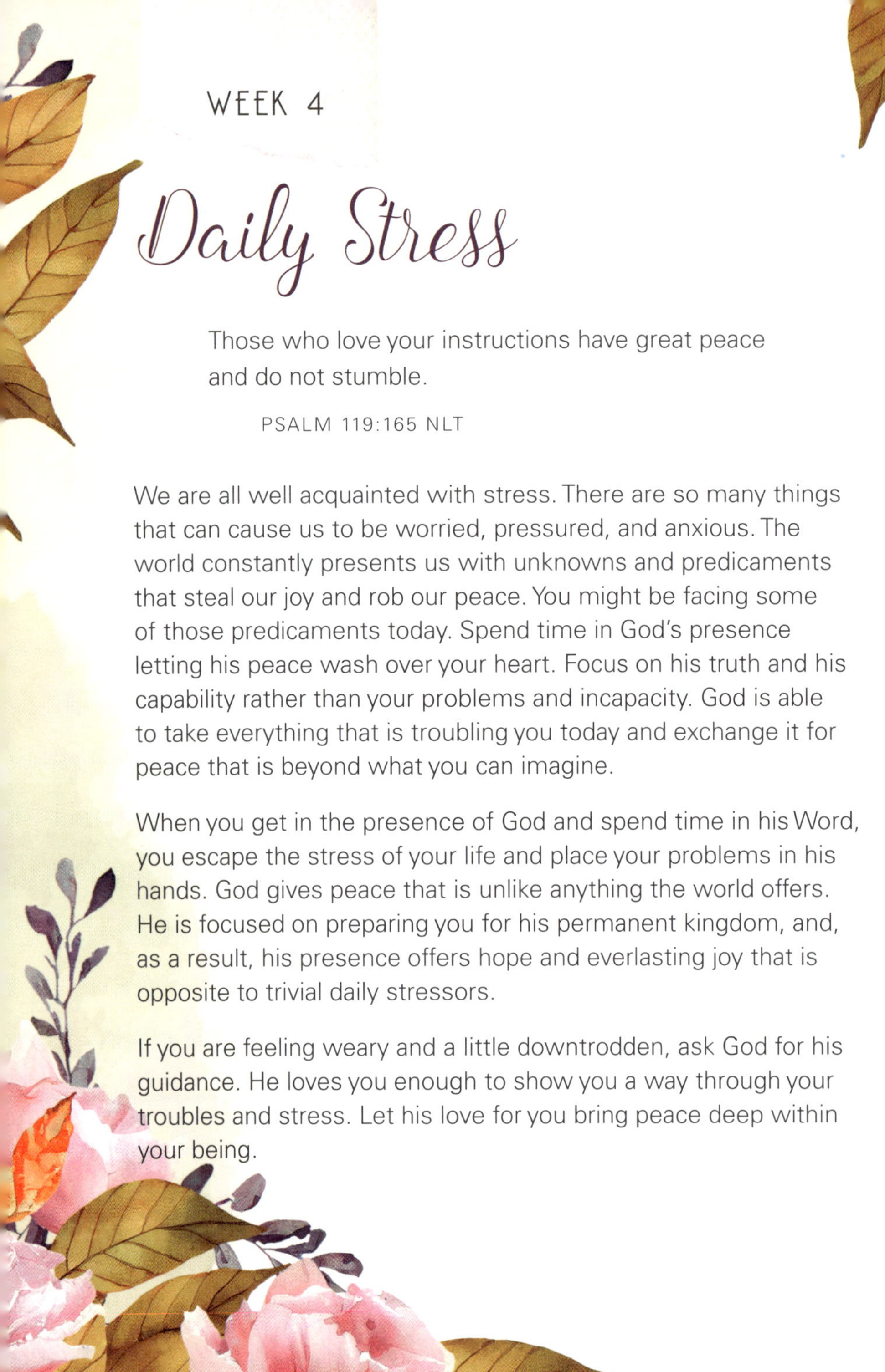

WEEK 4

Daily Stress

Those who love your instructions have great peace and do not stumble.

PSALM 119:165 NLT

We are all well acquainted with stress. There are so many things that can cause us to be worried, pressured, and anxious. The world constantly presents us with unknowns and predicaments that steal our joy and rob our peace. You might be facing some of those predicaments today. Spend time in God's presence letting his peace wash over your heart. Focus on his truth and his capability rather than your problems and incapacity. God is able to take everything that is troubling you today and exchange it for peace that is beyond what you can imagine.

When you get in the presence of God and spend time in his Word, you escape the stress of your life and place your problems in his hands. God gives peace that is unlike anything the world offers. He is focused on preparing you for his permanent kingdom, and, as a result, his presence offers hope and everlasting joy that is opposite to trivial daily stressors.

If you are feeling weary and a little downtrodden, ask God for his guidance. He loves you enough to show you a way through your troubles and stress. Let his love for you bring peace deep within your being.

How is God directing you through your worries and stress?

MY THOUGHTS

MY RESPONSE

The work of righteousness
will be peace,
And the effect of righteousness,
quietness and assurance forever.

ISAIAH 32:17 NJKV

To me, this Scripture feels most like (check one)

☐ A PROMISE ☐ AN INSTRUCTION ☐ A TRUTH

Here's how it impacts me...

Prayer

GRATITUDE

REQUESTS

WEEK 5

Loss of Control

My flesh and my heart fail;
But God is the strength of my heart
and my portion forever.

PSALM 73:26 NKJV

Have you ever had a moment where you've felt completely out of control? A car accident, a diagnosis, or some other frightening moment? There are instances when your own flesh fails you. You recognize in a flash that you are no longer in control of your own outcome, and it can be terrifying. In that moment, when control is lost and fear overcomes you, there is one thing you can know for certain. God is your strength, and he never loses control.

There are times when we feel strong and independent and there are times when we realize that we are completely dependent on others. God gave us gifts and strengths, but we are still finite creatures. At times we just have to admit that we can't do it all on our own.

The Psalmist recognized this and acknowledged that God is the source of strength. When your life, and the outcome of it, is ripped from your hands, it's still resting firmly in his grasp. He is your portion. He is your ration. He is enough. Release yourself into the control of the only one who will never lose control.

Reflection

What have you been trying to do all on your own? How can you rely more on God?

MY THOUGHTS

MY RESPONSE

In the day when I cried out,
You answered me,
And made me bold
with strength in my soul.

PSALM 138:3 NKJV

To me, this Scripture feels most like (check one)

☐ A PROMISE ☐ AN INSTRUCTION ☐ A TRUTH

Here's how it impacts me...

Prayer

GRATITUDE

REQUESTS

WEEK 6

> Do not throw away your confidence; it will be richly rewarded. You need to persevere so that when you have done the will of God, you will receive what he has promised.
>
> HEBREWS 10:35-36 NIV

Remember the early days of your relationship with God? Perhaps you were a child, full of wonder and excitement. Maybe you were an adult when you discovered his love, and it filled you to the brim with joy. Continue to persevere. Breathe in God's peace and rejoice in it. He will give you the strength you need to continue in him.

As you walk with Christ, life's ups and downs can get to you. The confidence that you placed in God to save you from yourself may waver. But he never does.

Don't lose heart! God promises to reward your faith. Place your trust in him, and he will help you persevere through any situation. When you feel like you may falter, turn to him and seek the joy that only he can provide.

Where is your confidence today?

MY THOUGHTS

MY RESPONSE

My beloved brethren, be steadfast, immovable, always abounding in the work of the Lord, knowing that your labor is not in vain in the Lord.

1 CORINTHIANS 15:58 NKJV

To me, this Scripture feels most like (check one)

☐ A PROMISE ☐ AN INSTRUCTION ☐ A TRUTH

Here's how it impacts me...

Prayer

GRATITUDE

REQUESTS

WEEK 7

Vulnerability

He gives us more grace. That is why Scripture says:
"God opposes the proud
but shows favor to the humble."

JAMES 4:6 NIV

Some of the most substantial and ultimately wonderful changes in our lives come from moments of vulnerability: laying our cards on the table, so to speak, and letting someone else know how much they really mean to us. But vulnerability takes one key ingredient: humility. And humility is not easy.

Isn't it sometimes easier to pretend that conflict never happened than to face the fact that we made a mistake and wronged another person? It's not always easy to humble ourselves and fight for the resolution in an argument especially when it means admitting our failures. The wrong kind of pride is not pretty. We are more likely to listen to those who are honest about their situation than those who are trying to make excuses for it.

Who are you in the face of conflict? Do you avoid apologizing in an attempt to save face? Does your pride get in the way of vulnerability, or are you willing and ready to humble yourself for restoration in your relationships? God says that he will give favor and wisdom to the humble.

Reflection

What can you do this week to humble yourself for the sake of a relationship?

MY THOUGHTS

MY RESPONSE

The LORD mocks the mockers
but is gracious to the humble.

PROVERBS 3:34 NLT

To me, this Scripture feels most like (check one)

☐ A PROMISE ☐ AN INSTRUCTION ☐ A TRUTH

Here's how it impacts me...

....

....

....

....

....

Prayer

GRATITUDE

REQUESTS

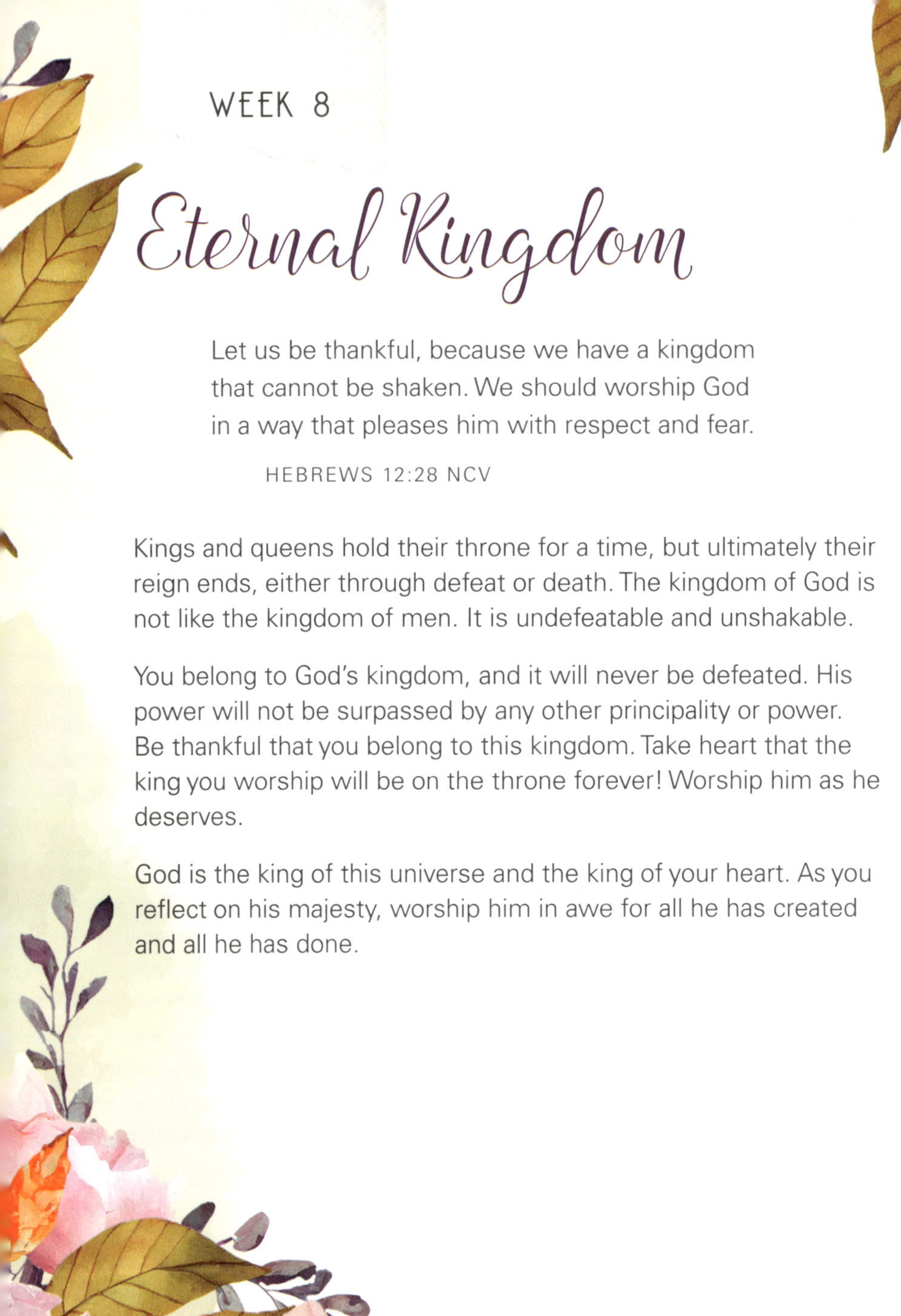

WEEK 8

Eternal Kingdom

Let us be thankful, because we have a kingdom that cannot be shaken. We should worship God in a way that pleases him with respect and fear.

HEBREWS 12:28 NCV

Kings and queens hold their throne for a time, but ultimately their reign ends, either through defeat or death. The kingdom of God is not like the kingdom of men. It is undefeatable and unshakable.

You belong to God's kingdom, and it will never be defeated. His power will not be surpassed by any other principality or power. Be thankful that you belong to this kingdom. Take heart that the king you worship will be on the throne forever! Worship him as he deserves.

God is the king of this universe and the king of your heart. As you reflect on his majesty, worship him in awe for all he has created and all he has done.

Reflection

What does an unshakable kingdom look like in your mind?

MY THOUGHTS

MY RESPONSE

"The God of heaven will set up a kingdom that will never be destroyed, nor will it be left to another people. It will crush all those kingdoms and bring them to an end, but it will itself endure forever."

DANIEL 2:44 NIV

To me, this Scripture feels most like (check one)

☐ A PROMISE ☐ AN INSTRUCTION ☐ A TRUTH

Here's how it impacts me...

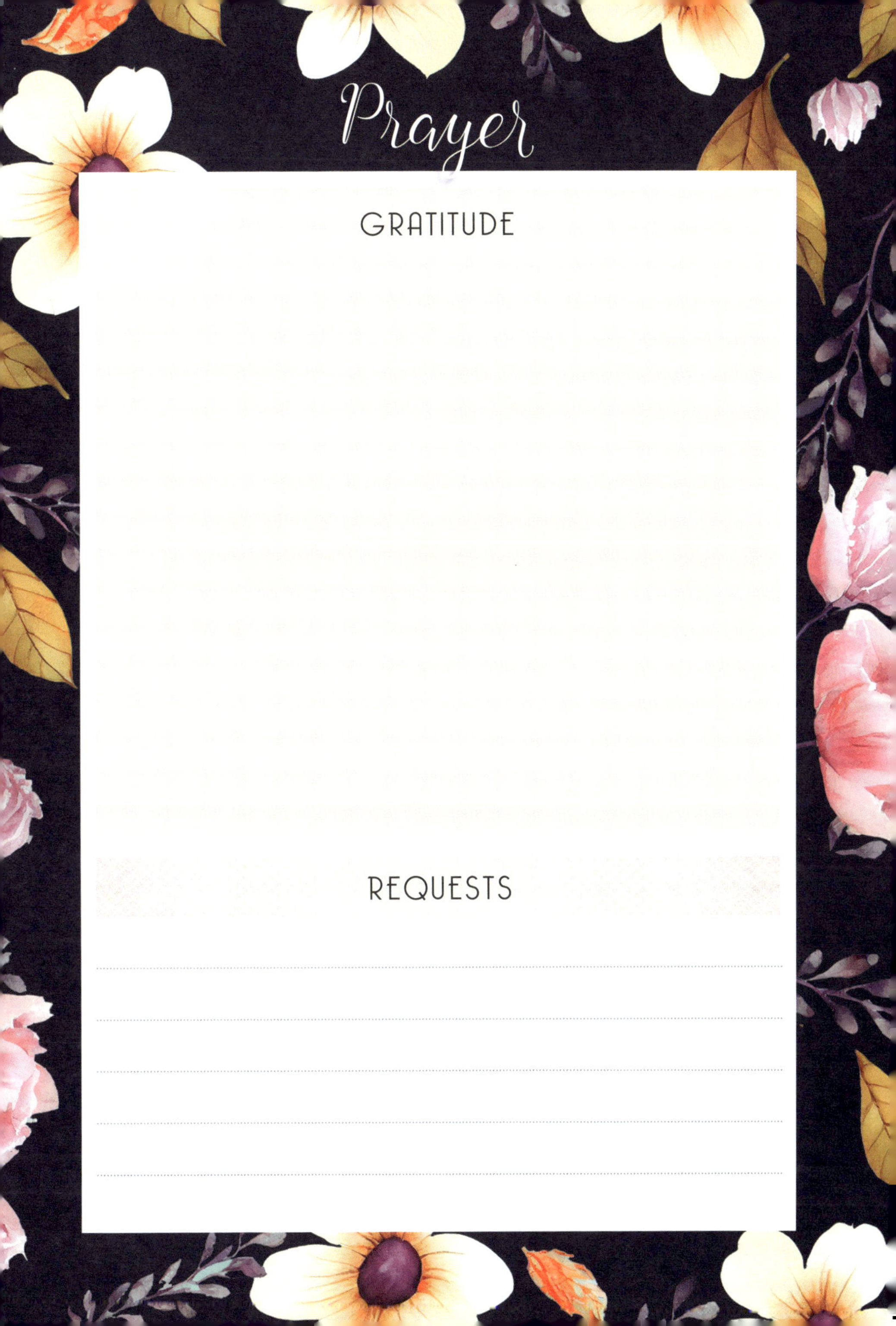

Prayer
GRATITUDE
REQUESTS

WEEK 9

Come Close

> Come close to God, and God will come close to you. Wash your hands, you sinners; purify your hearts, for your loyalty is divided between God and the world.
>
> JAMES 4:8 NLT

Do you ever feel like you can't feel God? Like you've lost sight of him somehow? Sometimes we aren't sure how to get back to that place where we feel his presence strongly and hear his voice clearly.

We go through seasons where we feel distant from God, but the beautiful truth is that he has never gone anywhere. He's in the same place he was the first time we met him. God is unchanging. His heart is always to be with us, and he never turns his back on his children. God will not push himself on you. He will not share his glory with another, and he will not try to compete with the world for your heart. But if you draw near to him, he will wrap you in the sweetness and power of his presence.

Where is your loyalty? Sometimes you may hardly have time to think about God, let alone allow him to be active and speaking. Let him renew your heart. Welcome him into your life above all other loves.

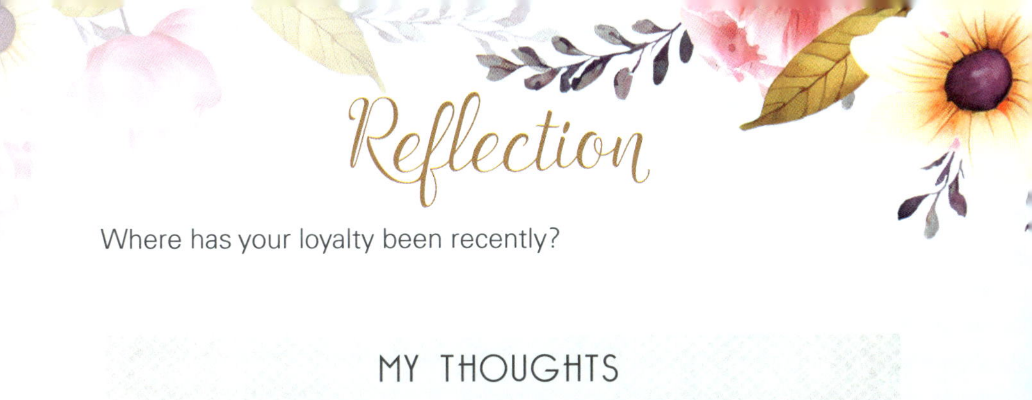

Reflection

Where has your loyalty been recently?

MY THOUGHTS

MY RESPONSE

The LORD is near to all
who call upon Him,
To all who call upon Him in truth.

PSALM 145:18 NKJV

To me, this Scripture feels most like (check one)

☐ A PROMISE ☐ AN INSTRUCTION ☐ A TRUTH

Here's how it impacts me...

Prayer

GRATITUDE

REQUESTS

WEEK 10

Promoted

> "His master said to him, 'Well done, good and faithful servant! You were faithful over a few things; I will put you in charge of many things. Share your master's joy.'"
>
> MATTHEW 25:23 CSB

Faithfulness brings exponential rewards in the kingdom of God. Not only do we receive the joy of obedience, but we receive more rewards from the trust God places on us. All of us can look forward to the day we stand before God, by his grace, having used our gifts well.

Here on earth, the application of increased trust can come into our lives in the forms of greater responsibility and influence. It could look like promotions and prestige: earthly responses to the glory God has placed upon us and we have ably carried.

When earthly blessings come your way, accept them with humbleness and gratitude. As you look ahead to the final day, use your gifts to further glorify God.

Reflection

What gifts do you use frequently?

MY THOUGHTS

MY RESPONSE

"Whoever serves me must follow me;
and where I am, my servant also will be.
My Father will honor the one who serves me."

JOHN 12:26 NIV

To me, this Scripture feels most like (check one)

☐ A PROMISE ☐ AN INSTRUCTION ☐ A TRUTH

Here's how it impacts me...

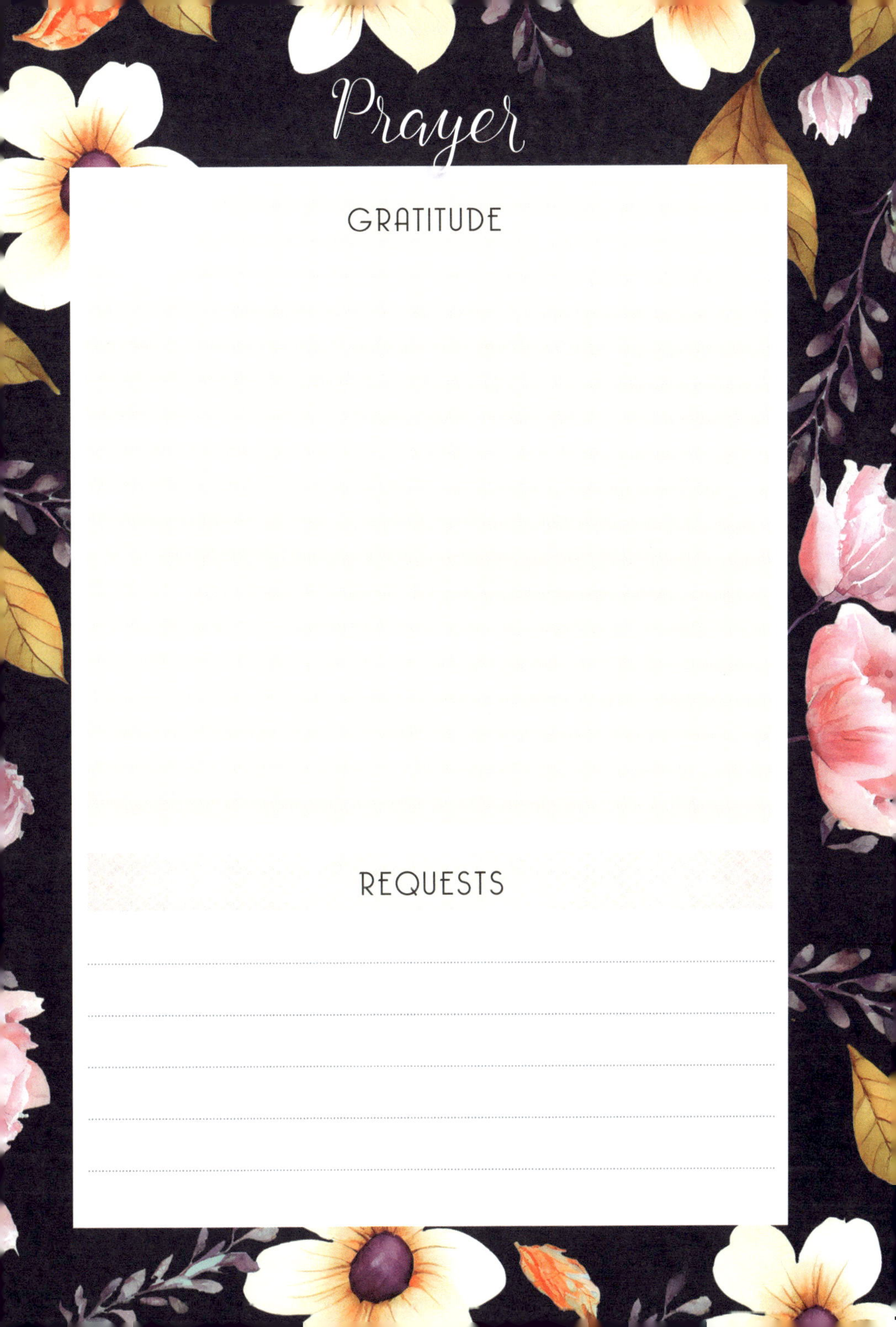

Prayer

GRATITUDE

REQUESTS

WEEK 11

Joy in Grief

Your promise revives me;
it comforts me in all my troubles.

PSALM 119:50 NLT

Grief is a strange thing. It shows up in the oddest of places. As time passes, it becomes threaded into your life in a subtle way you don't quite notice at first. When you smile and feel real joy but at the same moment tears spring to your eyes, that's when you know that grief is not absent even in happiness.

As time passes and life goes on, we must learn to bear all our varying emotions in sync. We can smile, we can laugh, and we can be perfectly happy, but the ache of grief is still there deep down. We don't forget it, but we don't betray that which we grieve by smiling either.

As a child of God, you have been promised a hope that has the power to revive you even in the most sorrowful of moments. And though your pain is real, deep, and sometimes overwhelming, your God is strong and able to lift you out of the deepest pit, and—even when it's hard to imagine—give you joy. Ask God for joy in the middle of your grief. Ask for moments of laughter and peace in places you would least expect to find them.

Reflection

What grief or trouble are you experiencing right now? How can you let God in?

MY THOUGHTS

MY RESPONSE

*When I am filled with cares,
your comfort brings me joy.*

PSALM 94:19 CSB

To me, this Scripture feels most like (check one)

☐ A PROMISE ☐ AN INSTRUCTION ☐ A TRUTH

Here's how it impacts me...

....

....

....

....

....

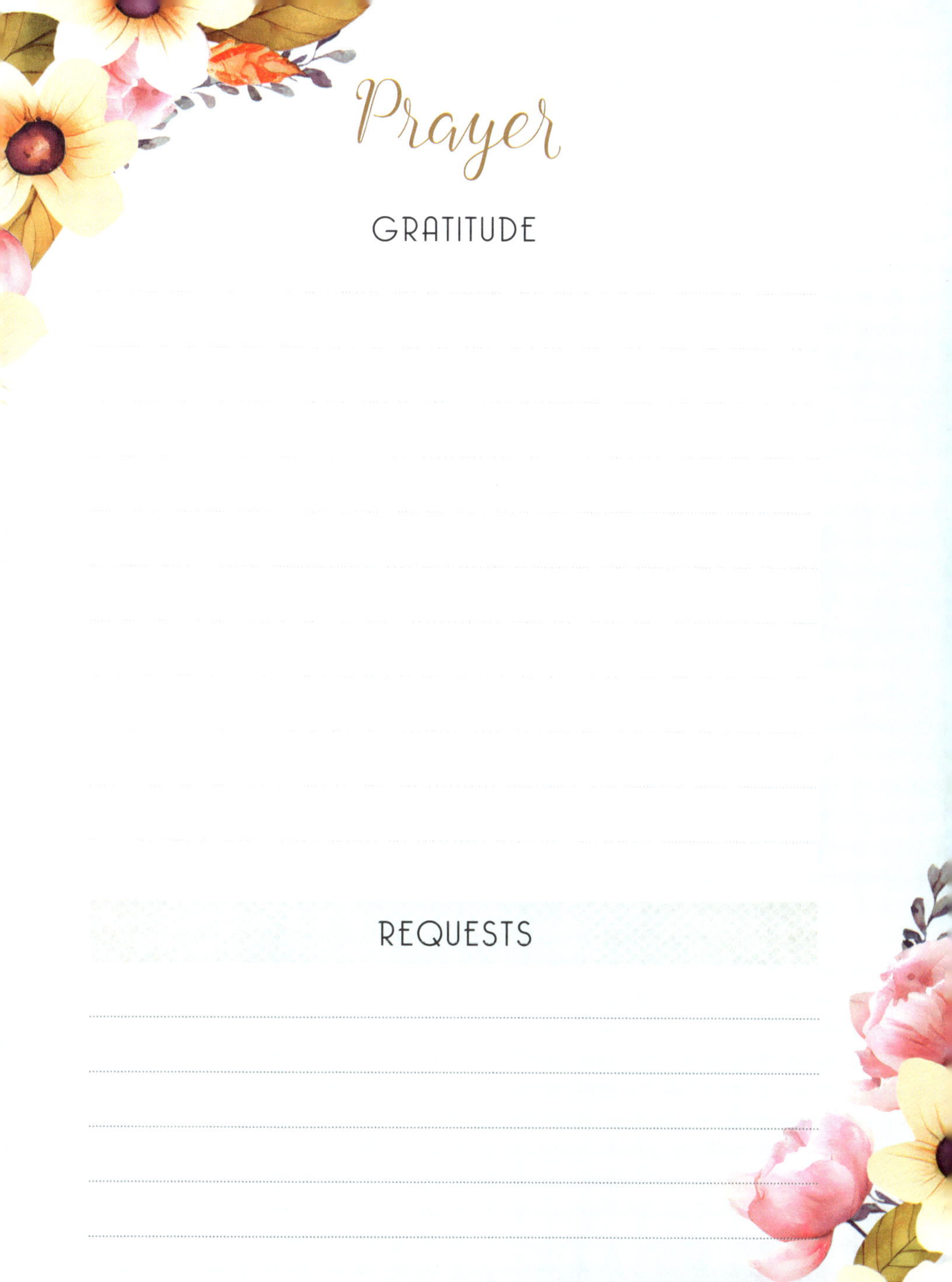

Prayer

GRATITUDE

REQUESTS

WEEK 12

Thirsty for Mercy

"Come, all you who are thirsty, come to the waters;
and you who have no money, come, buy and eat!
Come, buy wine and milk without money and
without cost."

ISAIAH 55:1 NIV

Money is used for what we want, but mostly for the things that we need—like food and even water. Imagine walking into a grocery store and being offered anything you want without having to pay a cent! This is a picture of the mercy that Jesus has shown all of us through his sacrifice.

We need God's mercy in the same way that we thirst for water. Wine and milk were expensive items in the time this was written, and to offer these free of charge would have been a great sacrifice.

What Christ did for you on the cross came at a great price, but it was all because of his great love for you. Embrace the free gift of forgiveness and rest in freedom. Think about God's amazing gifts as you go through each day. If that doesn't put a smile on your face, what else could?

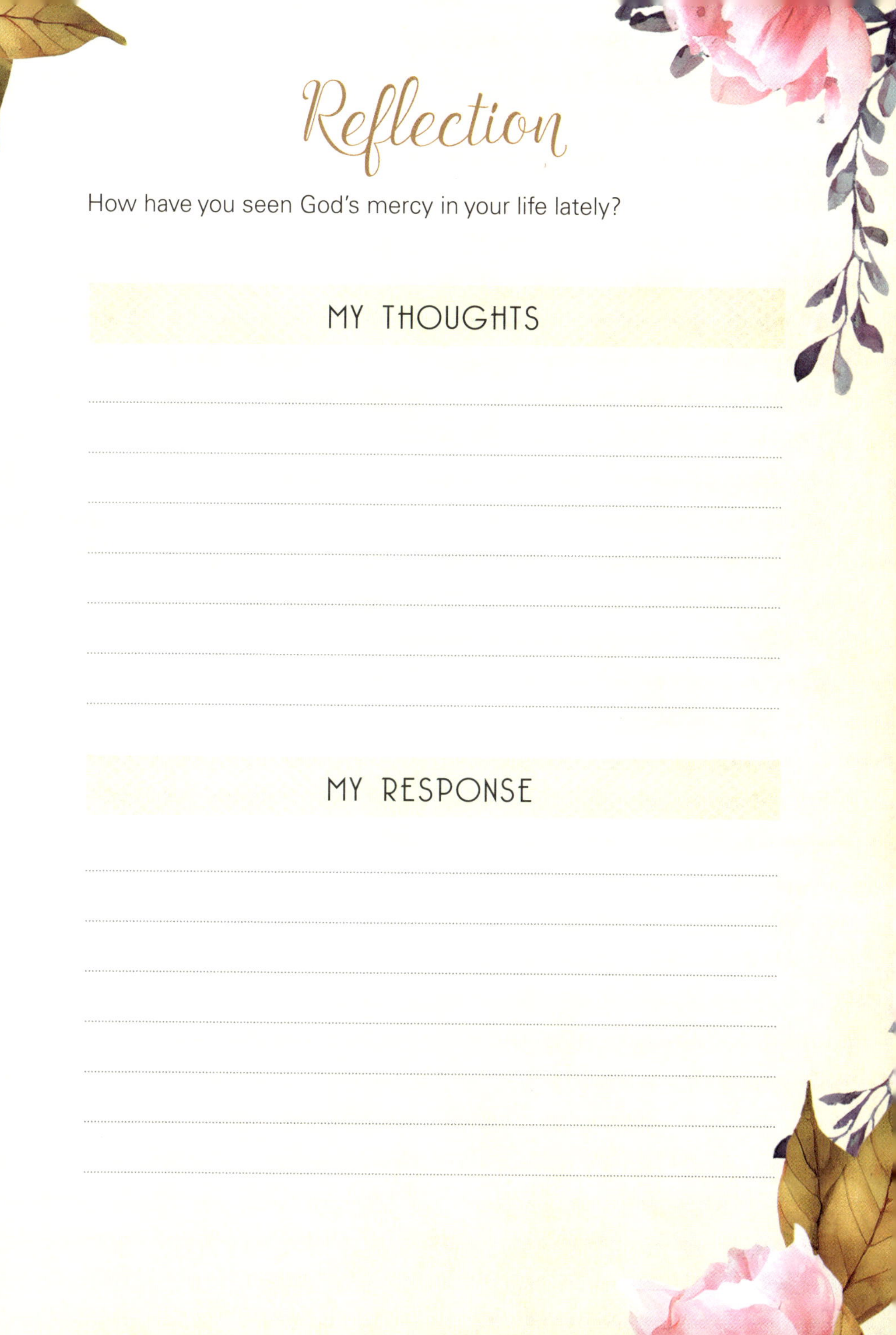

Reflection

How have you seen God's mercy in your life lately?

MY THOUGHTS

MY RESPONSE

"It is done. I am the Alpha and the Omega, the Beginning and the End. To the thirsty I will give water without cost from the spring of the water of life."

REVELATION 21:6 NIV

To me, this Scripture feels most like (check one)

☐ A PROMISE ☐ AN INSTRUCTION ☐ A TRUTH

Here's how it impacts me...

Prayer

GRATITUDE

REQUESTS

WEEK 13

Giving Thanks

Enter his gates with thanksgiving
and his courts with praise;
give thanks to him and praise his name.

PSALM 100:4 NIV

The morning alarms came too soon today. Whether they were in the form of children, an alarm clock, or a heavy heart that is restless, your slumber is over. Your mind immediately starts going over your to-do list for the day as you stumble through your morning routine. You glance at your watch. How can you already be running late?

It is at this moment that you must stop to thank God. That's right, actually stop what you are doing, get down on your knees (to ensure you are stopping), and thank him. Pausing to thank God gives him the honor he's due, but it also kisses your heart with peace and joy in the midst of busy morning routines.

A thankful heart prepares the way for you to connect rightly with God's heart. He isn't someone you use to get what you want. He is a sincere, loving provider for everything you will ever need. Thank him for this day, no matter how hectic, sad, or boring it might be. And if it looks to be a great day, tell him that too! He loves to hear your praise.

Reflection

What are you extra thankful for this week?

MY THOUGHTS

MY RESPONSE

Let the word of Christ dwell richly among you, in all wisdom teaching and admonishing one another through psalms, hymns, and spiritual songs, singing to God with gratitude in your hearts.

COLOSSIANS 3:16 CSB

To me, this Scripture feels most like (check one)

☐ A PROMISE ☐ AN INSTRUCTION ☐ A TRUTH

Here's how it impacts me...

....

....

....

....

....

Prayer

GRATITUDE

REQUESTS

WEEK 14

Relationships Matter

Spend time with the wise
and you will become wise,
but the friends of fools will suffer.

PROVERBS 13:20 NCV

Humans were created for relationships; we are hardwired to want and need others. Because of our design, friendships are vitally important, as is our walk with God. It is a widely known fact that friends either bring us up or drag us down.

Friends can either encourage or discourage us in our pursuit of godliness. As we seek counsel from our friends for the decisions we make in life, it is important that those friends are pushing us to follow Christ and not our own desires.

Your friends have the power to lead you closer to God or push you away from him. Surround yourself with people who will echo God's words to you rather than lead you off course with their advice. Evaluate yourself to make sure you are being the kind of friend who will lead others closer to Christ by your influence and your advice.

Who encourages you in your relationship with God? How do you encourage your friends?

MY THOUGHTS

MY RESPONSE

Do no be misled:
"Bad company corrupts good character."
Come back to your senses as you ought,
and stop sinning.

1 CORINTHIANS 15:33-34 NIV

To me, this Scripture feels most like (check one)

☐ A PROMISE ☐ AN INSTRUCTION ☐ A TRUTH

Here's how it impacts me...

Prayer

GRATITUDE

REQUESTS

WEEK 15

Scandalous Forgiveness

"Be on your guard. If your brother sins, rebuke him, and if he repents, forgive him. And if he sins against you seven times in a day, and comes back to you seven times, saying, 'I repent,' you must forgive him."

LUKE 17:3-4 CSB

There are few things worse than being unjustly wronged. It's not easy when you are hurt especially by someone close to you. A deep part of each of us cries out for justice. It's a God-given trait, meant to call us to stand in the gap for the hurting, the widow, the orphan; it's our longing for true religion. When we identify injustice, that longing rises up strongly. We feel pain, hurt, confusion, and pressure. And more than all those emotions, we feel the deep need to see justice served.

Forgive. Over and over again. This is the scandal of the gospel. The very essence of the Jesus we follow. If someone wrongs you, forgive them. If they do it again, forgive again. No matter what has taken place, the answer is the same—forgive.

Forgiveness is handing the hurt to God and leaving the judgment to him. No matter how hard it is to forgive someone who has hurt you, remember how much you have been forgiven. How can you extend any less grace than that which you have received?

Reflection

Who do you need to forgive today? How will you make sure that happens?

MY THOUGHTS

MY RESPONSE

"If you forgive other people when they sin against you, your heavenly Father will also forgive you."

MATTHEW 6:14 NIV

To me, this Scripture feels most like (check one)

☐ A PROMISE ☐ AN INSTRUCTION ☐ A TRUTH

Here's how it impacts me...

Prayer

GRATITUDE

REQUESTS

WEEK 16

Fully Alive

Without revelation people run wild,
but one who follows divine instruction
will be happy.

PROVERBS 29:18 CSB

Everyday living can suck the life right out of us. Somewhere in the middle of being stuck in traffic, sweeping floors, and brushing our teeth, we can forget to be alive. What does it mean to be alive rather than just to live? Not to only exist in life, but to know it, to understand it, to experience it—to *live* it. What would it be like freefalling from an airplane? Running through the grass barefoot with the sun on your face? Listening to the squeals of children as they are swept into their father's arms? What would it be like if we lived each moment in the spirit of those fully alive moments?

Without a reason for life, without purpose, we perish. We falter. We lose our way. We lose hope. We begin to casually exist instead of breathing in the reverence of a fully alive life.

Recast your vision daily. Open your mind and your heart to the vision that God has for you. If there are dreams he gave you that you've lost along the way, trust that they will be returned to you. God breathed life into you so that you could live it to the fullest.

Reflection

What do you need God to breathe life into?

MY THOUGHTS

MY RESPONSE

The one who looks intently into the perfect law of freedom and perseveres in it, and is not a forgetful hearer but a doer who works—this person will be blessed in what he does.

JAMES 1:25 CSB

To me, this Scripture feels most like (check one)

☐ A PROMISE ☐ AN INSTRUCTION ☐ A TRUTH

Here's how it impacts me...

Prayer

GRATITUDE

REQUESTS

WEEK 17

Never Too Late

> Indeed, the Lord's arm is not too weak to save,
> and his ear is not too deaf to hear.
>
> ISAIAH 59:1 CSB

Do you have regrets in your life? Things you wish you could take back? Things that you aren't proud of? You lay awake at night thinking about mistakes you've made and wonder if you've gone too far to ever get back.

When Jesus hung on the cross, there were two thieves hanging beside him. One of those thieves, as he hung in his final moments of life, asked Jesus for grace and a second chance. That thief—minutes before death—was given forgiveness and eternal life. The very same day he entered paradise as a forgiven and clean man. In light of his story, how can you ever say that it's too late to turn it all around?

If you feel like it's too late to change something in your life for the better, remember the story of the thief on the cross. There is always hope in Jesus. The God you serve is the God of second chances. That might sound cliché, but it couldn't be more true. His love has no end, and his grace knows no boundary. It is never too late for you to follow him with your life.

Reflection

What do you need to be saved from today?

MY THOUGHTS

MY RESPONSE

"I will provide for their needs
before they ask,
and I will help them while they
are still asking for help."

ISAIAH 65:24 NCV

To me, this Scripture feels most like (check one)

☐ A PROMISE ☐ AN INSTRUCTION ☐ A TRUTH

Here's how it impacts me...

Prayer

GRATITUDE

REQUESTS

WEEK 18

> "I love you people with a love that will last forever.
> That is why I have continued showing you kindness.
> People of Israel, I will build you up again,
> and you will be rebuilt.
> You will pick up your tambourines again
> and dance with those who are joyful."
>
> JEREMIAH 31:3-4 NCV

We were originally created to bear the mark of our Creator. We were masterfully designed to reflect his image and to reveal his glory. The corruption of sin has masked us, disguising our initial intended purpose. When we respond to salvation and give ourselves back to God, he begins reworking us to once again appear as he intended.

Sanctification is a process that can be painful. But its end result is beautiful. God empties our hearts of the things that could never satisfy us to make room for himself—the only thing that will always satisfy.

Perhaps today you feel like God has taken a wrecking ball to your life. He has flattened everything you had—your desires, your interests, your pursuits—but fear not. He will rebuild you. He is creating a masterpiece that will bring him glory and honor. Everything God removes he will restore to mirror the image of his likeness which is your intended created purpose.

What do you feel has been broken in your life? Can you trust God to rebuild you?

MY THOUGHTS

MY RESPONSE

*From eternity to eternity
the LORD's faithful love is
toward those who fear him,
and his righteousness
toward the grandchildren.*

PSALM 103:17 CSB

To me, this Scripture feels most like (check one)

☐ A PROMISE ☐ AN INSTRUCTION ☐ A TRUTH

Here's how it impacts me...

Prayer

GRATITUDE

REQUESTS

WEEK 19

New Life

> We died and were buried with Christ by baptism. And just as Christ was raised from the dead by the glorious power of the Father, now we also may live new lives.
>
> ROMANS 6:4 NLT

The entire human race is living on borrowed time. We spend our lives with the innate knowledge that we never know when it will all end for us. Death comes, as it always does, to every man.

When it came to Jesus, death didn't have the final say. And in that death—the one death that represented all humanity—the greatest form of life was born. The gospel truth is that Jesus' death wasn't just a man's life ending on a cross. It was the death to end all deaths. Jesus died and took the full wrath of a righteous God upon himself, so our death sentences would no longer be ours to serve. And the story doesn't end there. The most glorious part of all is his resurrection: his conquering of death, and the ultimate display of power, glory, victory, and grace.

The whole point of the gospel summed up in one life giving phrase is this: you can have new life. Life that doesn't run out, expire, or end. This beautiful truth isn't just a charming thought; it's your reality as a Christian. By accepting the finished story of the gospel, you are written into the best ending in existence. Life is yours—glorious, powerful life. Ponder that for a while.

Reflection

What impacts you the most about the saving work of Christ?

MY THOUGHTS

MY RESPONSE

If anyone belongs to Christ, there is a new creation. The old things have gone; everything is made new!

2 CORINTHIANS 5:17 NCV

To me, this Scripture feels most like (check one)

☐ A PROMISE ☐ AN INSTRUCTION ☐ A TRUTH

Here's how it impacts me...

....

....

....

....

....

Prayer

GRATITUDE

REQUESTS

WEEK 20

Heaven's Promise

"He will wipe away all tears from their eyes, and there shall be no more death, nor sorrow, nor crying, nor pain. All that has gone forever."

REVELATION 21:4 NLT

When terrible things happen in this world, people cry out to God in desperation. They ask how he could have let it happen. How could the one who is in control of everything possibly be good when there is so much hardship? But when we look at the system of heaven, we realize that God never intended for us to have sorrow, pain, or death. All these things only exist as a result of man's sin.

When the kingdom of heaven is established on earth, we will live as God intended. All wrong will be righted and all pain will disappear. It is good to live and love with eternity's values in mind. On some days, it can be the difference between despair and hope.

As a child of God, you know that any pain you have in this life is temporary because your eternal home will be devoid of it all. When the pain and sadness of the world threatens to overwhelm you, cling to the promise of heaven and the hope that one day every tear will be wiped from your eyes.

Reflection

What do you feel when you think about all wrongs being righted and all pain being gone?

MY THOUGHTS

MY RESPONSE

He will destroy death forever.
The Lord GOD will wipe away
every tear from every face.
He will take away the shame of
his people from the earth.

ISAIAH 25:8 NCV

To me, this Scripture feels most like (check one)

☐ A PROMISE ☐ AN INSTRUCTION ☐ A TRUTH

Here's how it impacts me...

Prayer

GRATITUDE

REQUESTS

WEEK 21

Already In

Those who respect the Lord will live
and be satisfied, unbothered by trouble.

PROVERBS 19:23 NCV

As advertisements go, Proverbs 19:23 puts forth a rather persuasive pitch for joining our lives to God's. Satisfaction? Yes, please! Unbothered by trouble? Let us in! Here's the best part of all: we already signed. We're already in. The day we fell in love with Jesus and asked him into our hearts, all this and more was ours. To claim it, we need only remain in his love. To experience it, we need only give the Father our awe.

When we are reclined on the beach, hearing gentle waves rhythmically hit the shore, the ocean doesn't seem particularly fearsome. Jumping from a ship into twelve-foot swells with no land in sight? It's hard to imagine anything more terrifying. It's all a matter of perspective. From land, it's easy to forget the ocean's vastness and power. From the center, it's impossible to think of anything else.

This is what it means to fear God. To fear him is to respect him: to remember his vastness, to stand in awe of his power. Let us remain at the center of our faith, constantly aware of all he can, has, and will do, and find our secure rest there.

Reflection

How can the fear of God bring you a feeling of safety?

MY THOUGHTS

MY RESPONSE

The eye of the LORD
is on those who fear him,
on those who hope in his steadfast love.

PSALM 33:18 ESV

To me, this Scripture feels most like (check one)

☐ A PROMISE ☐ AN INSTRUCTION ☐ A TRUTH

Here's how it impacts me...

Prayer

GRATITUDE

REQUESTS

WEEK 22

Heart Directions

> May the Lord direct your hearts to the love of God and to the steadfastness of Christ.
>
> 2 THESSALONIANS 3:5 ESV

Popular culture says the key to happiness is to follow your heart. The idea is that by pursuing our passions we're most likely to end up in a good place. It seems like lovely advice, but only as long as we're sure our hearts know the way. Could your heart use directions from time to time? The heart's wants can be based on selfish, unhealthy, or irresponsible desires. God's heart is steady and true. He knows exactly where we need to go. His unwavering love for us will make certain we get there.

Visit any public venue and you're likely to see children sprinting away from their parents. Their excitement can't be contained in their little bodies. They bolt because they are so certain they know where to go. We hear their harried parents call out, "Slow down!" Whether by allowing them to temporarily believe they are lost, or by explaining the potential dangers of running away, parents will try to teach children to stay close.

How often do you charge ahead, running headlong without looking back? You know the Lord has plans for you. When you catch a glimpse of what's next, don't bolt. Look left and right, check the rearview mirror, slow down, and listen. Let the Father guide each step.

Where do you think God is leading you?

MY THOUGHTS

MY RESPONSE

If we hope for what we do not see,
we wait for it with patience.

ROMANS 8:25 ESV

To me, this Scripture feels most like (check one)

☐ A PROMISE ☐ AN INSTRUCTION ☐ A TRUTH

Here's how it impacts me...

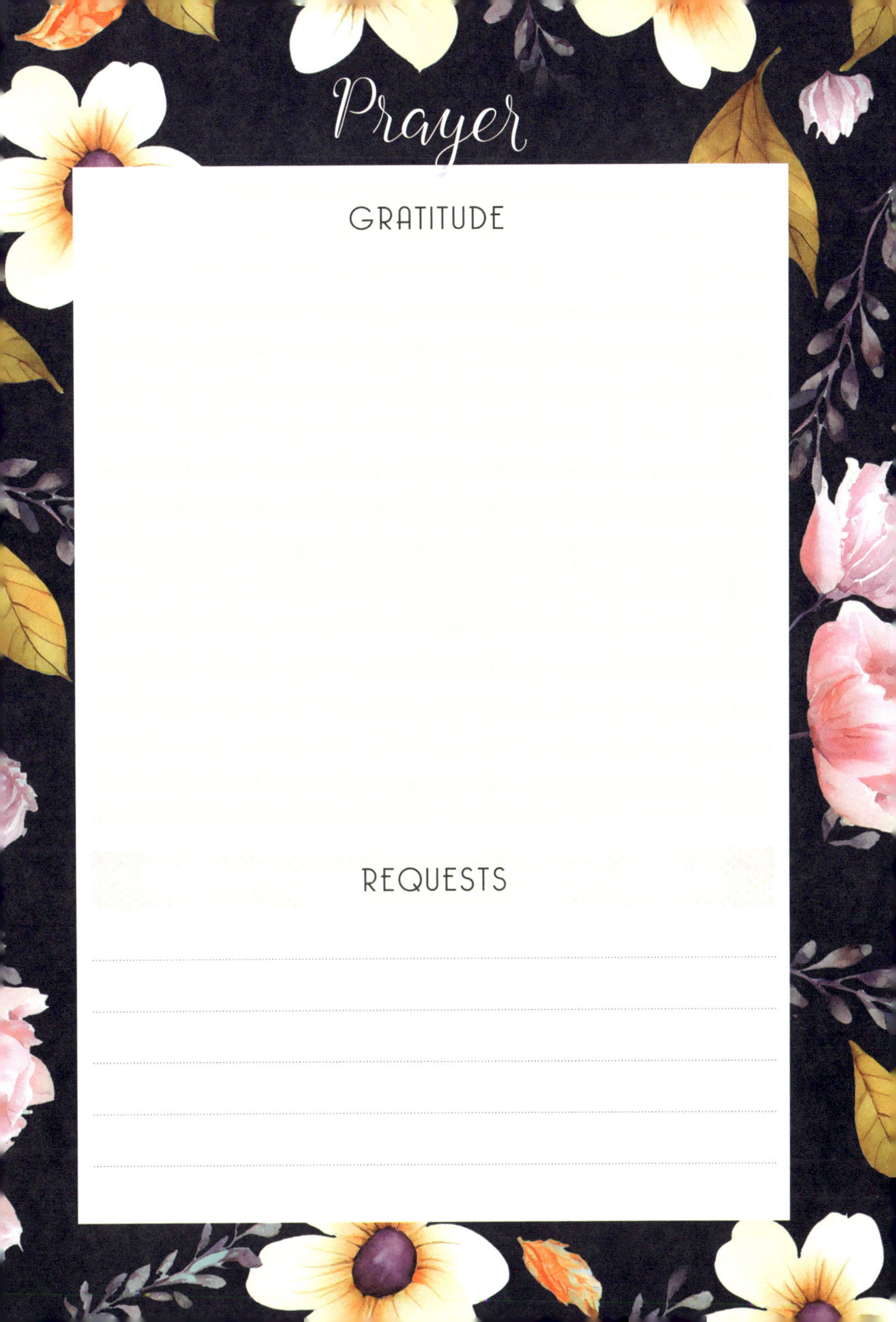

Prayer

GRATITUDE

REQUESTS

WEEK 23

Deeper Roots

"Still other seed fell on good soil, where it produced a crop—a hundred, sixty, or thirty times what was sown. Whoever has ears, let them hear."

MATTHEW 13:8-9 NIV

Calla lilies are beautiful flowers with wide, spotted leaves, thick stems, and bold colors. Year after year, you can watch the stunning leaves appear, and anticipate the gorgeous flowers, and then be disappointed when nothing more happens. Perhaps the soil is the problem? Calla lilies can be very particular.

It's a great picture of Jesus' parable of the sower and the seeds. Some seeds fall on rocky soil, and while God's Word is received, it doesn't take firm root and quickly withers at the sign of hardship. The seeds that are established in good soil, where the roots can go deep, not only survive, but they also bear fruit.

Do you hope to see more depth in your relationship with Jesus? Do you want others to see God's beauty displayed through your life? Be encouraged to hear the words of Jesus and then allow those words to penetrate your heart deeply until you understand them. Plant yourself in fertile soil and watch the beauty that emerges.

Reflection

How do the words of Jesus affect the way you live?

MY THOUGHTS

MY RESPONSE

It was majestic in beauty,
with its spreading boughs,
for its roots went down
to abundant waters.

EZEKIEL 31:7 NIV

To me, this Scripture feels most like (check one)

☐ A PROMISE ☐ AN INSTRUCTION ☐ A TRUTH

Here's how it impacts me...

GRATITUDE

REQUESTS

WEEK 24

Awakening the Sun

Praise him, sun and moon.
Praise him, all you shining stars.
Let them praise the Lord,
because they were created by his command.

PSALM 148: 3, 5 NCV

Spring is a gorgeous time of year. As the sun warms the ground, snow melts, buds open, and the earth appears to come back to life after a deep slumber.

Just as we appreciate the beauty of the seasons, God has a fine eye for loveliness too. He is the ultimate painter, creating a beautiful canvas all over the world as it awakes. He wants each of us to be embraced in the warmth of the sun as we are reminded of his love and care.

Look up! Turn your face toward the sun. Let its warmth rest on you. God is working in all things. Like the sunlight touches every corner of the earth, the Lord moves in every area of your life. Allow him to do his work in you today. Take time to notice the ways in which he is touching you with his warm embrace.

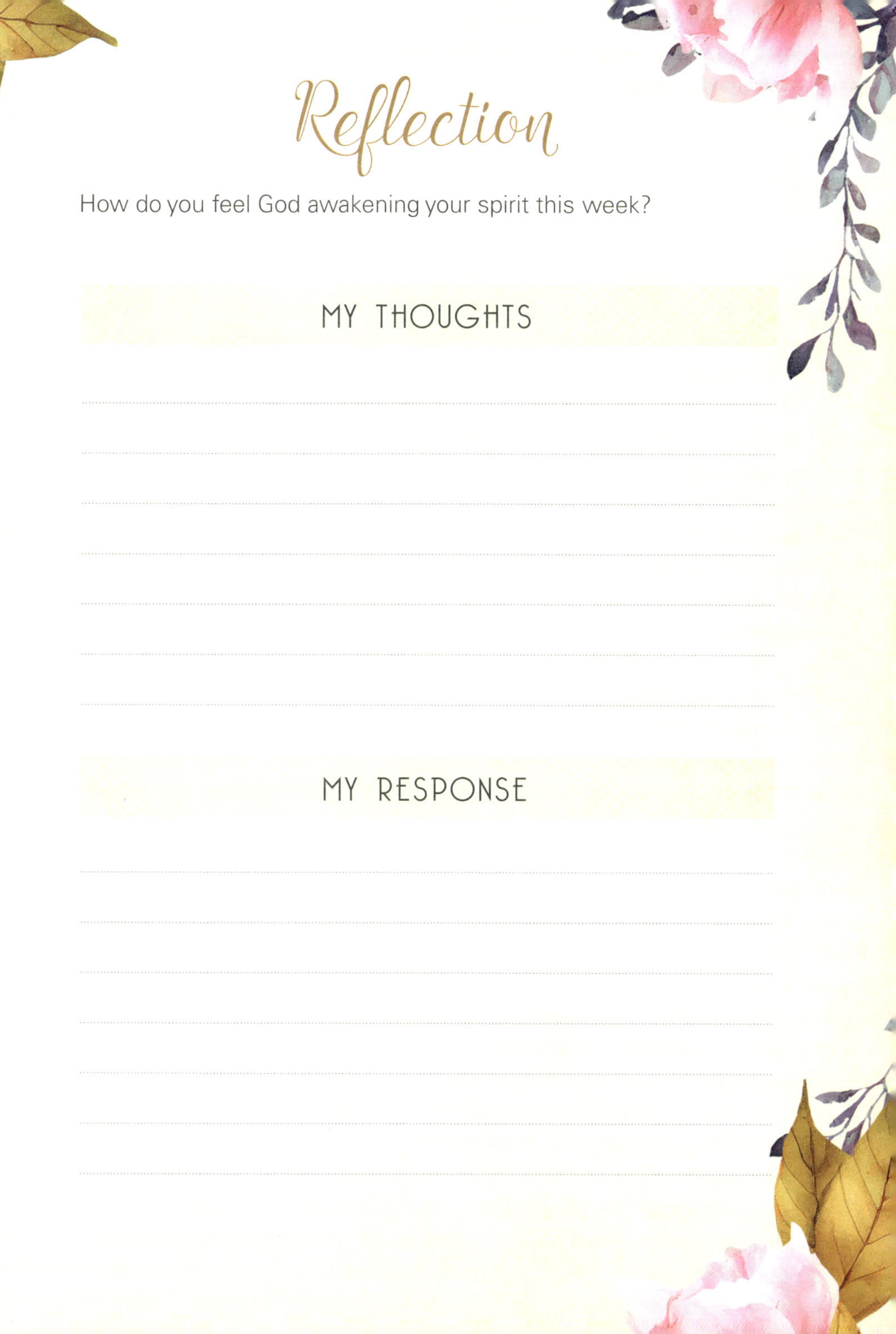

Reflection

How do you feel God awakening your spirit this week?

MY THOUGHTS

MY RESPONSE

From the rising of the sun
to its going down
The LORD's name is to be praised.

PSALM 113:3 NKJV

To me, this Scripture feels most like (check one)

☐ A PROMISE ☐ AN INSTRUCTION ☐ A TRUTH

Here's how it impacts me...

....

....

....

....

....

Prayer

GRATITUDE

REQUESTS

WEEK 25

Most Beautiful

I have asked one thing from the LORD;
it is what I desire:
to dwell in the house of the LORD
all the days of my life.
gazing on the beauty of the LORD
and seeking him in his temple.

PSALM 27:4 CSB

If there is one thing most people can appreciate, it's something pretty. Shiny things easily catch our attention, and we seek to surround ourselves with beauty. There is much beauty to be found in our natural world.

There is nothing wrong with finding loveliness, but if there is one thing that is more beautiful than anything else, it is God himself. His love, his mercy, his grace, and his understanding is nothing short of breathtaking.

Don't miss the beauty of the Lord today. Seek it. It's there to be found! You've been created to enjoy all that is exquisite, beautiful, and captivating. Give in to that desire and find it in him! Once you have discovered the allure of it, you will find that nothing is more fetching than the Lord in his love.

Reflection

Where do you find beauty in creation? How can you discover the beauty of God?

MY THOUGHTS

MY RESPONSE

*His invisible attributes, that is,
his eternal power and divine nature,
have been clearly seen since the creation
of the world, being understood through
what he has made.*

ROMANS 1:20 CSB

To me, this Scripture feels most like (check one)

☐ A PROMISE ☐ AN INSTRUCTION ☐ A TRUTH

Here's how it impacts me...

GRATITUDE

REQUESTS

WEEK 26

> My beloved spoke and said to me,
> "Arise my darling,
> my beautiful one, come with me."
>
> SONG OF SOLOMON 2:10 NIV

Some say that romance is dead. It's not for God. He is the lover of our souls. He desires nothing more than time with his creation! It can be a little uncomfortable to have his gaze so intently on us though. We're nothing special, after all! Not beauty queens, academic scholars, or athletic prodigies of any kind. We might not be musical, or crafty, or organized. Our house might be a mess, and we could probably use a manicure.

Do you feel a bit squeamish under such an adoring gaze? There is good news for you! You are, in fact, his beautiful one! And he does want to bring you out of the cold winter. He's finished the watering season, and it is finally—*finally*—time to rejoice in the season of renewal.

The time has come. He is calling you, regardless of how unworthy you may think you are. Will you arise and come away with your beloved? He is waiting for you!

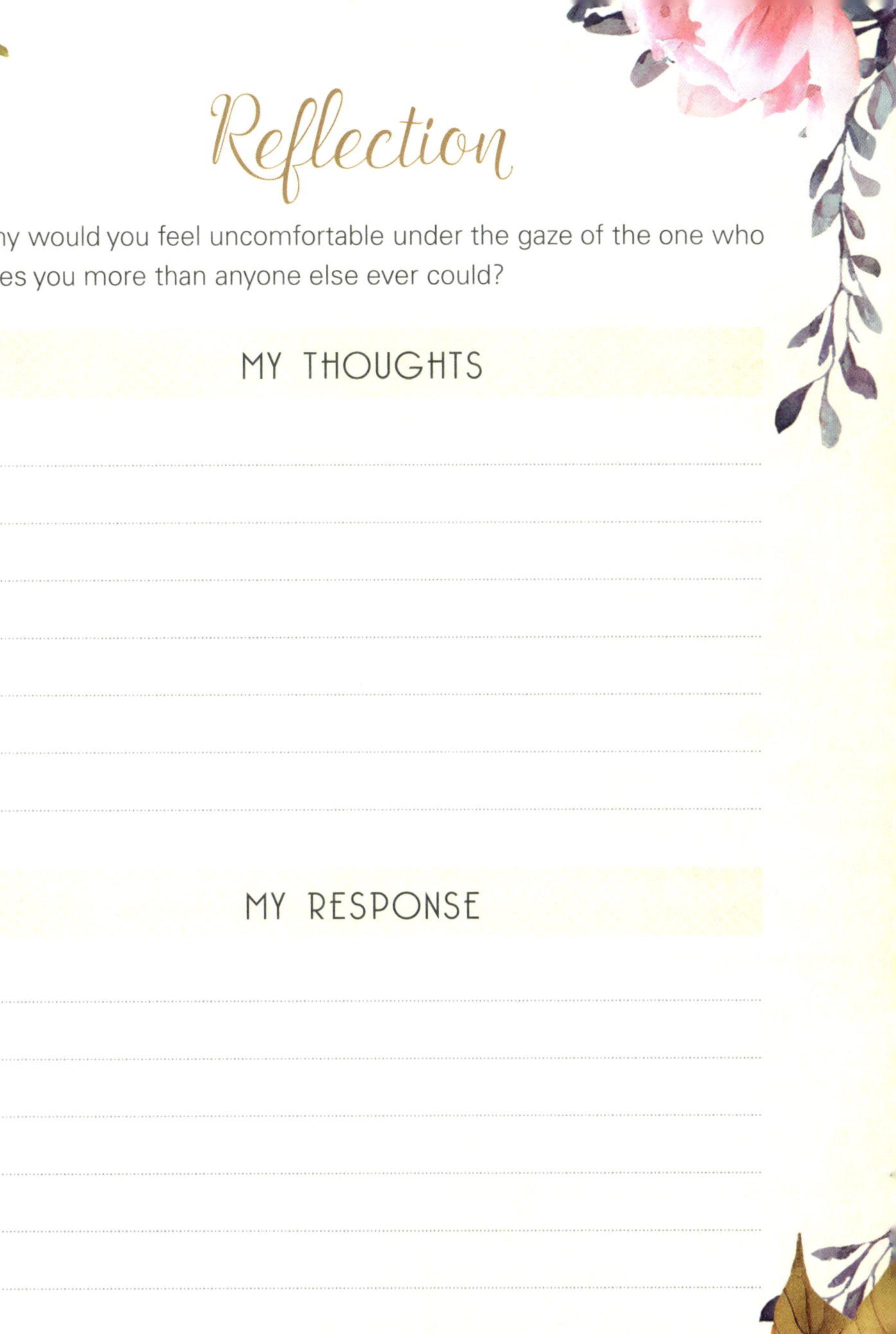

Reflection

Why would you feel uncomfortable under the gaze of the one who loves you more than anyone else ever could?

MY THOUGHTS

MY RESPONSE

Jesus said, "Let's go off by ourselves to a quiet place and rest awhile."

MARK 6:31 NLT

To me, this Scripture feels most like (check one)

☐ A PROMISE ☐ AN INSTRUCTION ☐ A TRUTH

Here's how it impacts me...

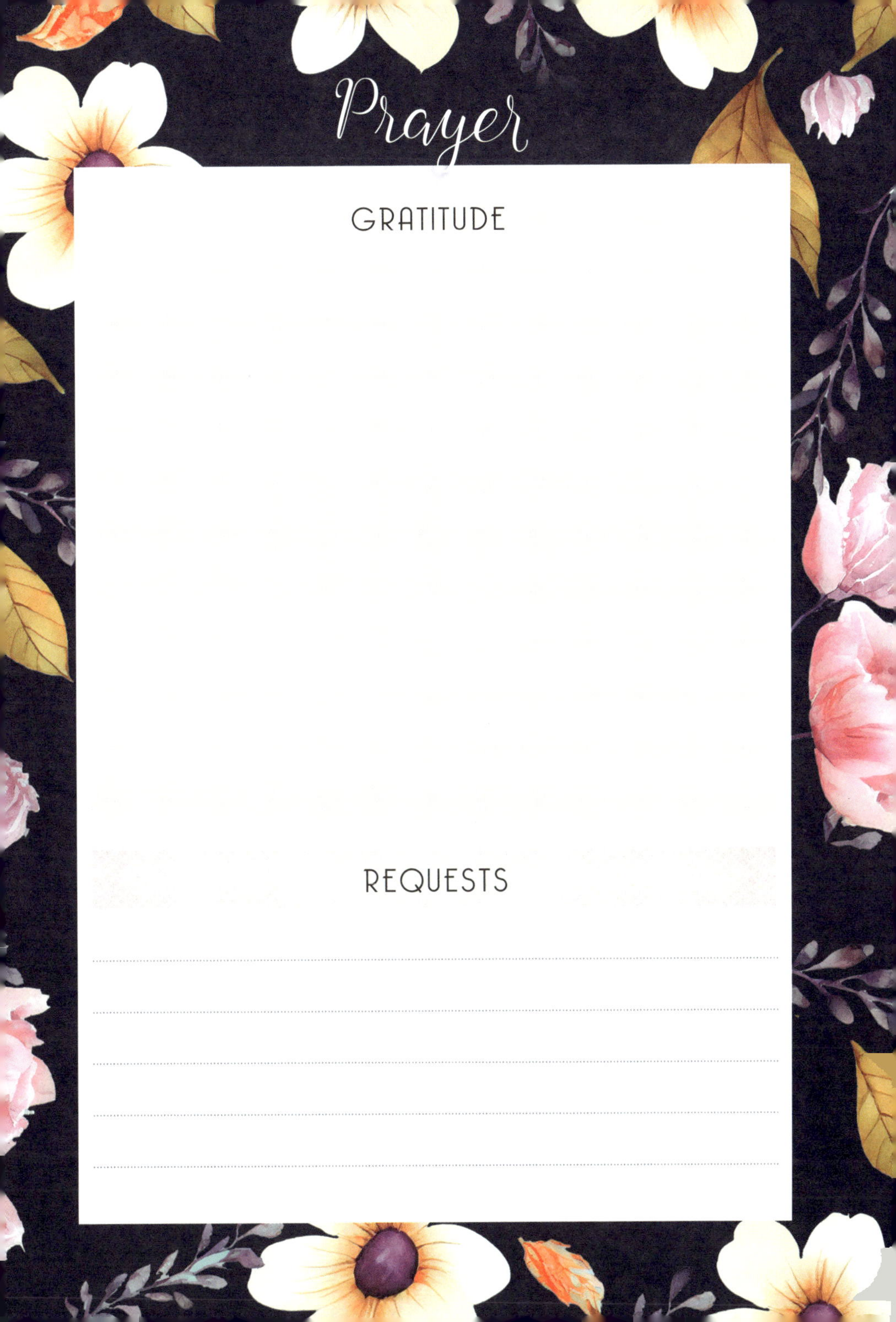

Prayer

GRATITUDE

REQUESTS

WEEK 27

Hidden Beauty

> We do not lose heart. Though our outer self is wasting away, our inner self is being renewed day by day.
>
> 2 CORINTHIANS 4:16 ESV

Beauty is a powerful influencer. We are constantly bombarded with images and messages of what beauty is and what it should be. Even if we are confident in who we are, it can still be difficult not to give in to the subtle thoughts of not being good enough. The awful truth about outward beauty is that no matter how much time, attention, and investment we put into it, that beauty can never really last. Our appearance inevitably changes over time, and our physical beauty does fade.

In a world where we are constantly told to beautify ourselves so we will be noticed, the concept of adorning the hidden person of the heart sounds almost make-believe. But what it comes down to is the truth that the most important opinion we should seek is the opinion of our Creator. When we step away from the distraction of the media circus and all the lies it's told us, the truth becomes clear.

You were made to delight the heart of God. Nothing delights him more than your heart turned toward him and clothed in the imperishable beauty of a peaceful spirit flowing with gentleness, kindness, and goodness.

Reflection

How can you actively shut out the opinions of beauty as defined by the world around you?

MY THOUGHTS

MY RESPONSE

Charm is deceptive,
and beauty does not last;
but a woman who fears the LORD
will be greatly praised.

PROVERBS 31:30 NLT

To me, this Scripture feels most like (check one)

☐ A PROMISE ☐ AN INSTRUCTION ☐ A TRUTH

Here's how it impacts me...

Prayer

GRATITUDE

REQUESTS

WEEK 28

Layers

> I am sure of this, that he who started a good work in you will carry it on to completion until the day of Christ Jesus.
>
> PHILIPPIANS 1:6 CSB

The art of a painting lies not in what you see, but in the process that has gone into making it what it has become. Usually a painting begins with inspiration: an idea or emotion that wants to be expressed. It proceeds with sketching, color, texture, and variations in between. A painter rarely produces exactly what they originally pictured.

Our life with God can be like a painting. It begins with our faith. Our belief in Jesus sets up our canvas, but the Scriptures call us to add to the depth of our faith by applying colors of goodness, knowledge, and self-control. The beauty emerges as we add perseverance, godliness, affection, and love. These things take time to develop. They can involve mistakes, and they can end up making us look very different than how we started.

Jesus has begun a good work in you. Have faith in his saving grace. Make the effort to become more beautiful by applying goodness, perseverance, and love to your life.

What do you feel God has been painting on the layered canvas of your life?

MY THOUGHTS

MY RESPONSE

God is working in you to help you want to do and be able to do what pleases him.

PHILIPPIANS 2:13 NCV

To me, this Scripture feels most like (check one)

☐ A PROMISE ☐ AN INSTRUCTION ☐ A TRUTH

Here's how it impacts me...

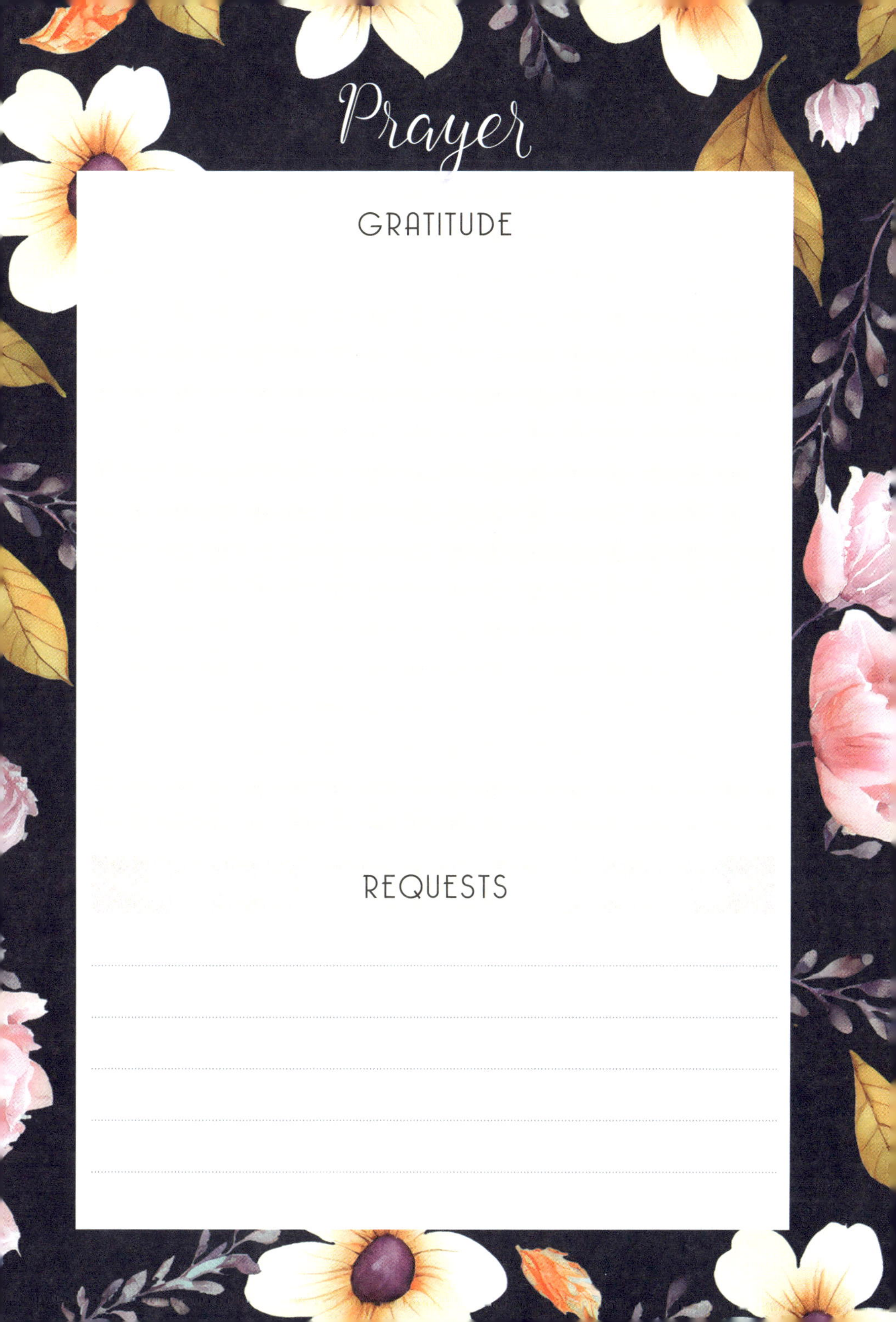

Prayer

GRATITUDE

REQUESTS

WEEK 29

Refining Process

> You rejoice in this, even though now for a short time, if necessary, you suffer grief in various trials so that the proven character of your faith—more valuable than gold which, though perishable, is refined by fire—may result in praise, glory, and honor at the revelation of Jesus Christ.
>
> 1 PETER 1:6-7 CSB

Creating a diamond is, for the transforming coal, a long and painful process. Simple carbon undergoes an immense refining pressure that produces a wholly new creation. We might just see a cloudy rock at this stage, but there is another refining step to be taken. After the stonecutter does his work, a precise shining diamond emerges: magnificent, glittering, brilliant.

When we endure hardship, the long and painful process can seem unfair. But our life stories are written by a compassionate Creator who is crafting a masterpiece. He is refining us, like the diamond, into something entirely beyond our imagination. And we can rejoice in the beauty he is creating. We may not see it now, but it's coming soon.

Let God show you the emerging beauty under the surface of the hardships you face. You will come out of the situation stronger and brighter and shining for God if you submit to his process and trust his skilled and loving hands.

Reflection

What trial is God refining you through right now?

MY THOUGHTS

MY RESPONSE

I consider that our present sufferings are not worth comparing with the glory that will be revealed in us.

ROMANS 8:18 NIV

To me, this Scripture feels most like (check one)

☐ A PROMISE ☐ AN INSTRUCTION ☐ A TRUTH

Here's how it impacts me...

Prayer

GRATITUDE

REQUESTS

WEEK 30

Follow the Arrow

> Your ears shall hear a word behind you, saying,
> "This is the way, walk in it,"
> Whenever you turn to the right hand
> Or whenever you turn to the left.
>
> ISAIAH 30:21 NKJV

Decisions, decisions. It seems a week never goes by without our needing to make at least one important choice. Whether job related, relationship motivated, or something as seemingly innocent as how to spend a free Friday, wouldn't it be nice to have an arrow pointing us in the right direction—especially if we are in danger of making a wrong turn?

According to the Word, we have exactly that. When we truly desire to walk the path God sets us on, and when we earnestly seek his voice, he promises to lead us in the right direction. His ever-present Spirit is right there, ready to put us back on the path each time we wander off.

Consider the decisions before you right now. Who do you turn to for guidance? Lay your options before God and listen for his voice.

What big decisions are you trying to make? How can you let God into your process?

MY THOUGHTS

MY RESPONSE

"I will instruct you and teach you
in the way you should go;
I will guide you with My eye."

PSALM 32:8 NKJV

To me, this Scripture feels most like (check one)

☐ A PROMISE ☐ AN INSTRUCTION ☐ A TRUTH

Here's how it impacts me...

Prayer

GRATITUDE

REQUESTS

WEEK 31

Known and Loved

> I am convinced that neither death nor life, neither angels nor demons, neither the present nor the future, nor any powers, neither height nor depth, nor anything else in all creation, will be able to separate us from the love of God that is in Christ Jesus our Lord.
>
> ROMANS 8:38-39 NIV

It's good to be loved, isn't it? What feeling really compares to knowing someone has run through the rain, cancelled an international flight, driven all night—for you? Even if you've never experienced it, you may have imagined it in your heart. Or else you've had the realization that you would move heaven and earth for the one you love. Whether husband, child, parent, sibling, or dear friend, to love and be loved deeply may be the best feeling there is.

How much love you have given or received is a mere sampling of the way Jesus feels about you. You are cherished: loved beyond reason or measure. The one who really can move heaven and earth would do so in a heartbeat for you.

Let these incredible words wash over you as you realize there is nothing—absolutely nothing—Jesus wouldn't do for you. Can you feel his love toward you today?

Reflection

How can you be convinced that nothing can stand in the way of God's love for you?

MY THOUGHTS

MY RESPONSE

*"I give them eternal life,
and they shall never perish;
neither shall anyone snatch them
out of My hand."*

JOHN 10:28 NKJV

To me, this Scripture feels most like (check one)

☐ A PROMISE ☐ AN INSTRUCTION ☐ A TRUTH

Here's how it impacts me...

Prayer

GRATITUDE

REQUESTS

WEEK 32

Untroubled Heart

"I leave you peace; my peace I give you. I do not give it to you as the world does. So don't let your hearts be troubled or afraid."

JOHN 14:27 NCV

I can't get a moment's peace. Sound familiar? We all go through seasons where it seems every corner hides a new challenge to our serenity, assuming we've actually achieved any semblance of serenity in the first place. Why is it so hard to find peace in this world? Because we're looking *in this world.*

After his resurrection, before Jesus ascended into heaven, he left his disciples with something they'd never had before—peace. More specifically, he gave them *his* peace: a gift not of this world. Whatever the world can offer us can also be taken from us. Any security, happiness, or temporary reprieve from suffering is just that: temporary. Only the things of heaven are permanent and cannot be taken away.

Do not *let* your heart be troubled, Jesus says. This means you have a choice. Share the things with him that threaten your peace, and then remember they have no hold on you. You are his, and his peace is yours.

Reflection

How can you choose peace in your situation today?

MY THOUGHTS

MY RESPONSE

God's peace, which is so great we cannot understand it, will keep your hearts and minds in Christ Jesus.

PHILIPPIANS 4:7 NCV

To me, this Scripture feels most like (check one)

☐ A PROMISE ☐ AN INSTRUCTION ☐ A TRUTH

Here's how it impacts me...

....

....

....

....

....

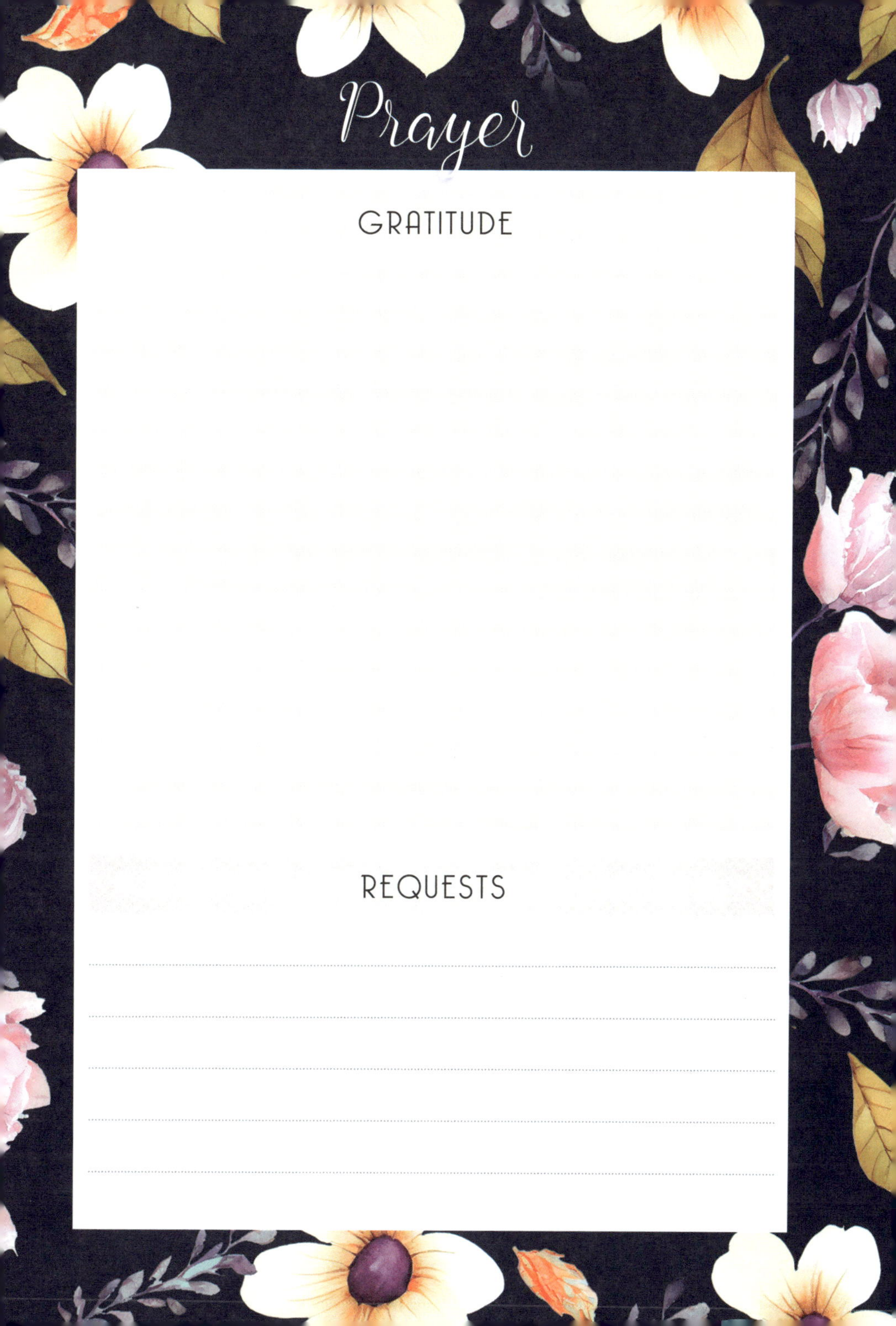

Prayer

GRATITUDE

REQUESTS

WEEK 33

The Patience Pit

> I waited patiently for the Lord,
> and he turned to me and heard my cry for help.
>
> PSALM 40:1 CSB

We're not that good at waiting for anything these days. Yet, the reality is that waiting is a necessary part of life. We wait for people, we wait for events, and we wait for desires to be fulfilled. But do we recognize that waiting might also apply to our emotional lives? Do we hold on to hope that we can be rescued from anxiety or depression?

King David described himself as being in a pit of miry clay, likely another of his despairing moments perhaps even on reflection of his sins. He needed to be rescued, not necessarily from his enemies, but from his state of mind. David says he *waited patiently,* understanding that he might not be instantly rescued. And he trusted that God alone would save him.

Do you feel as though your emotions are on slippery ground or that your thoughts are stuck in the miry clay? Are you willing to wait patiently for the great rescuer to lift you up and place your feet on solid ground? Take a moment today to ask God for his help, recognize the necessity of waiting, and trust him for the rescue.

Reflection

What have you been waiting for? Is patience still evident in your waiting?

MY THOUGHTS

MY RESPONSE

He brought me up from a desolate pit,
out of the muddy clay,
and set my feet on a rock,
making my steps secure.

PSALM 40:2 CSB

To me, this Scripture feels most like (check one)

☐ A PROMISE ☐ AN INSTRUCTION ☐ A TRUTH

Here's how it impacts me...

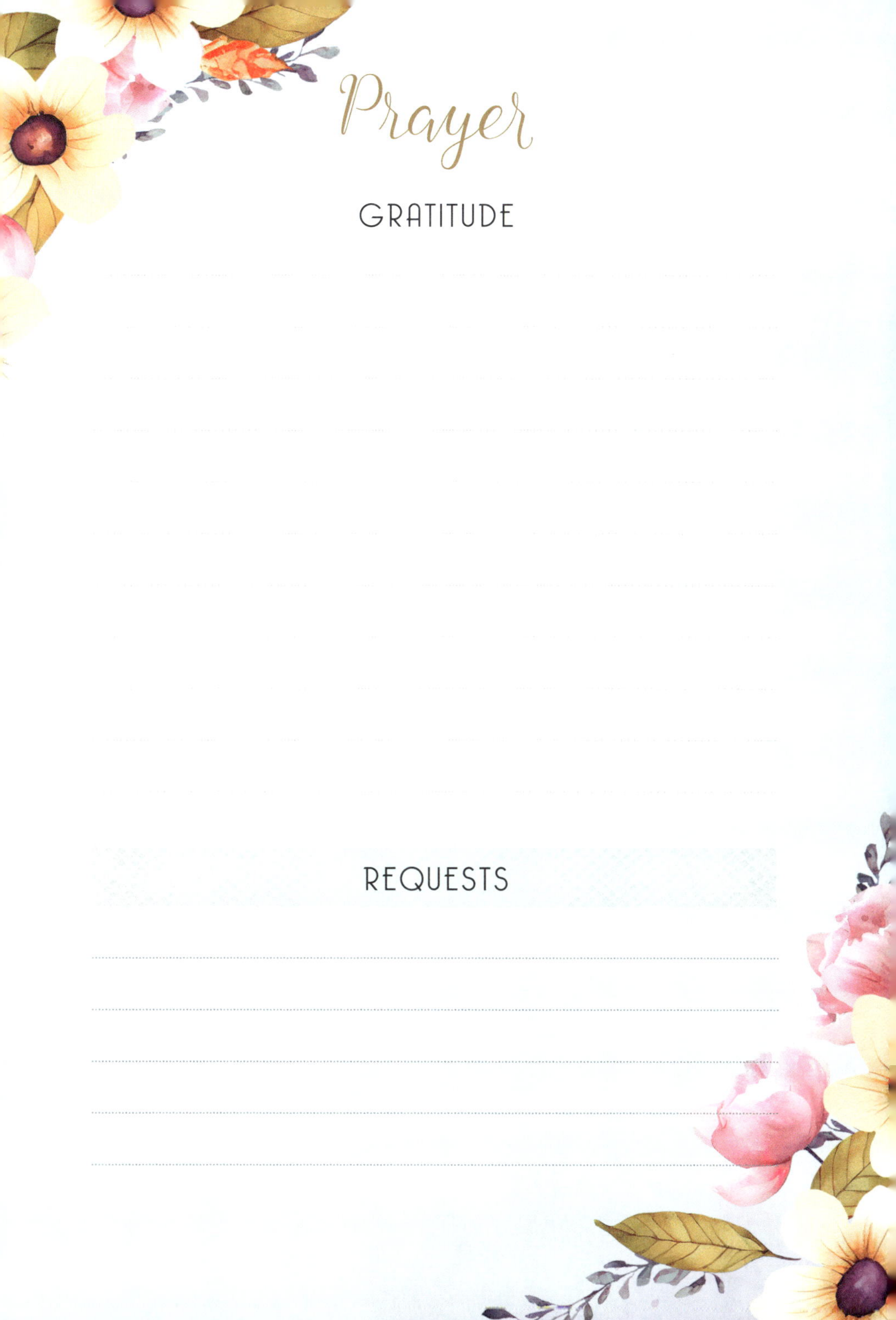

Prayer

GRATITUDE

REQUESTS

WEEK 34

Creatures of Habit

> Do not be conformed to this world, but be transformed by the renewal of your mind, that by testing you may discern what is the will of God, what is good and acceptable and perfect.
>
> ROMANS 12:2 ESV

Wake up. Make your bed. Get dressed. Drink coffee. Not always in that order, but you can guarantee that many do those things every single morning. They might also bite their nails, anger easily, and stay up too late. Patterns are hard to break. We are, after all, creatures of habit, and unfortunately not all of those habits are good.

What do you do when you are confronted with a habit that is not positive? Do you recognize when you rely on something just because it makes you feel accepted, comforted, or in control? Sometimes we aren't even conscious of our habits until we try to give them up.

Scripture says that establishing the right pattern begins with the renewing of our minds. This means that we must first acknowledge the need for change, and then submit our way of thinking to resemble that of Christ.

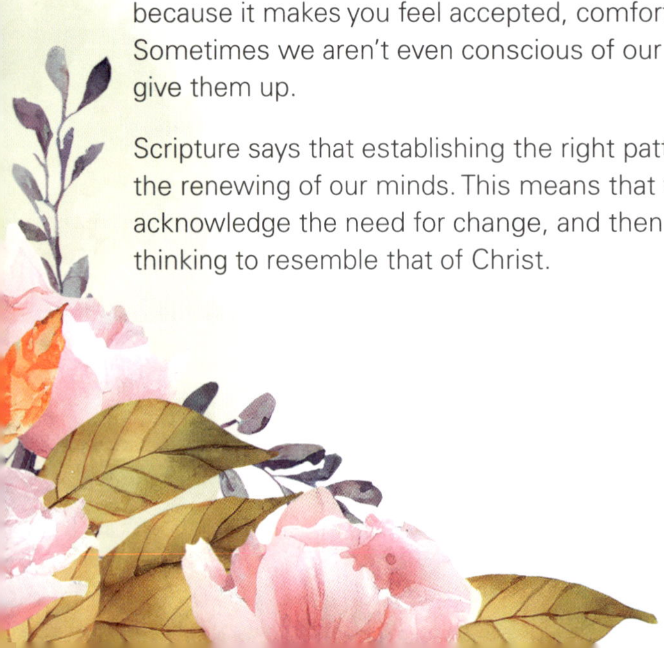

What habits are you trying to break? Can you trust God today to show you his will as you submit your worldly patterns to him?

MY THOUGHTS

MY RESPONSE

You have left your old sinful life and the things you did before. You have begun to live the new life, in which you are being made new and are becoming like the One who made you.

COLOSSIANS 3:9-10 NCV

To me, this Scripture feels most like (check one)

☐ A PROMISE ☐ AN INSTRUCTION ☐ A TRUTH

Here's how it impacts me...

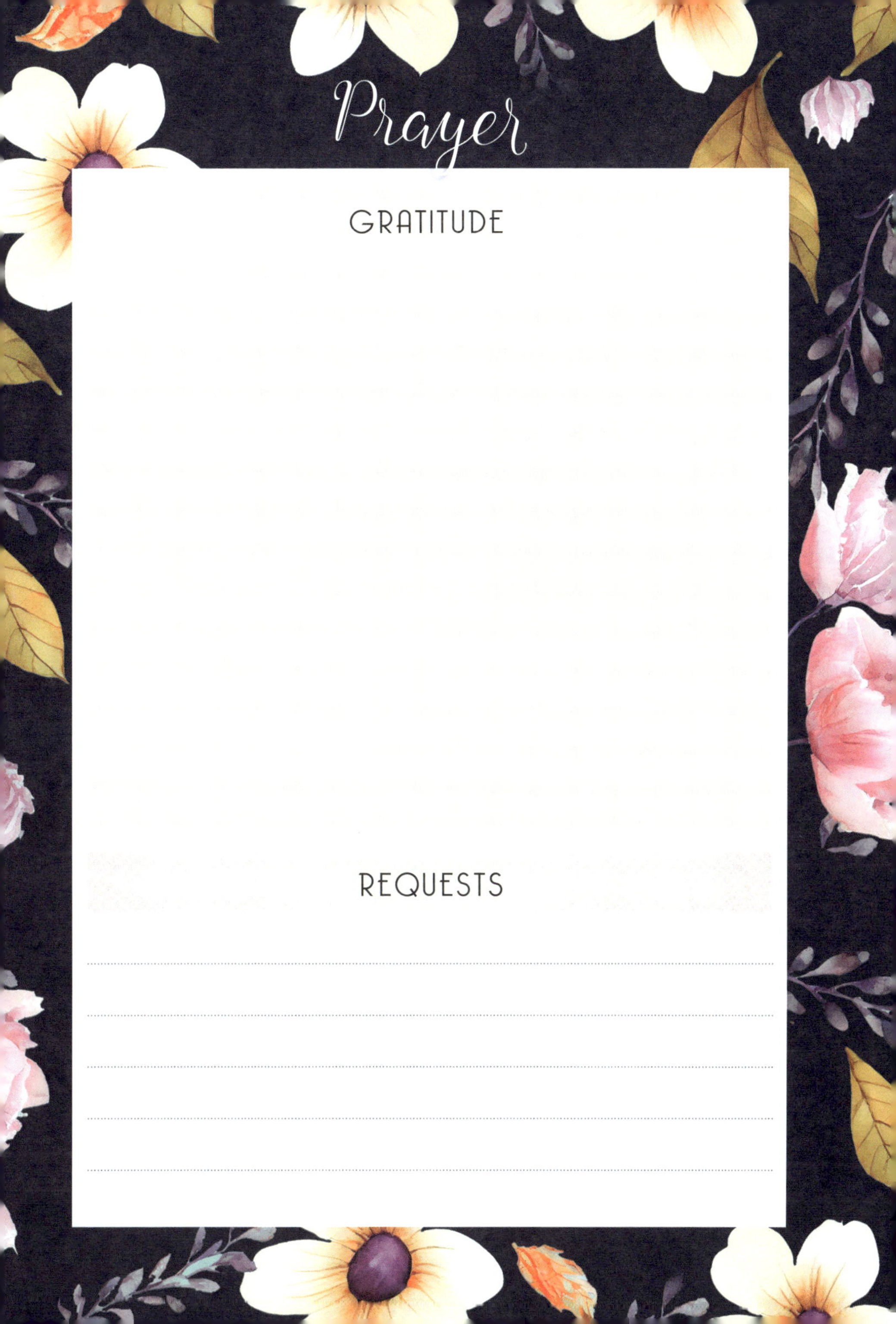
Prayer
GRATITUDE
REQUESTS

WEEK 35

Fully Trusting

> Trust in the LORD with all your heart,
> And lean not on your own understanding;
> In all your ways acknowledge Him,
> And He shall direct your paths.
>
> PROVERBS 3:5-6 NKJV

Trust can be a hard word to put into action mostly because our experience with others tells us that we can be sorely disappointed. People let us down in many ways. We can even be disappointed in ourselves.

Remember the trust game that involved standing with eyes closed and falling back into the hands of a few peers in hopes that they would catch you? There was risk involved in that game, and it didn't always turn out well. Nothing can truly be guaranteed in this life, can it? It depends on where you place your trust.

God watches over us, cares for us, and is involved in our lives. When we acknowledge that every good thing comes from him, our faith is strengthened, and we are able to trust him more. Make a point of noticing how God directs your paths this week and thank him for being trustworthy.

Reflection

How do you put your trust in God? What are you asking him to direct in your life?

MY THOUGHTS

MY RESPONSE

Commit everything you do to the LORD.
Trust him, and he will help you.

PSALM 37:5 NLT

To me, this Scripture feels most like (check one)

☐ A PROMISE ☐ AN INSTRUCTION ☐ A TRUTH

Here's how it impacts me...

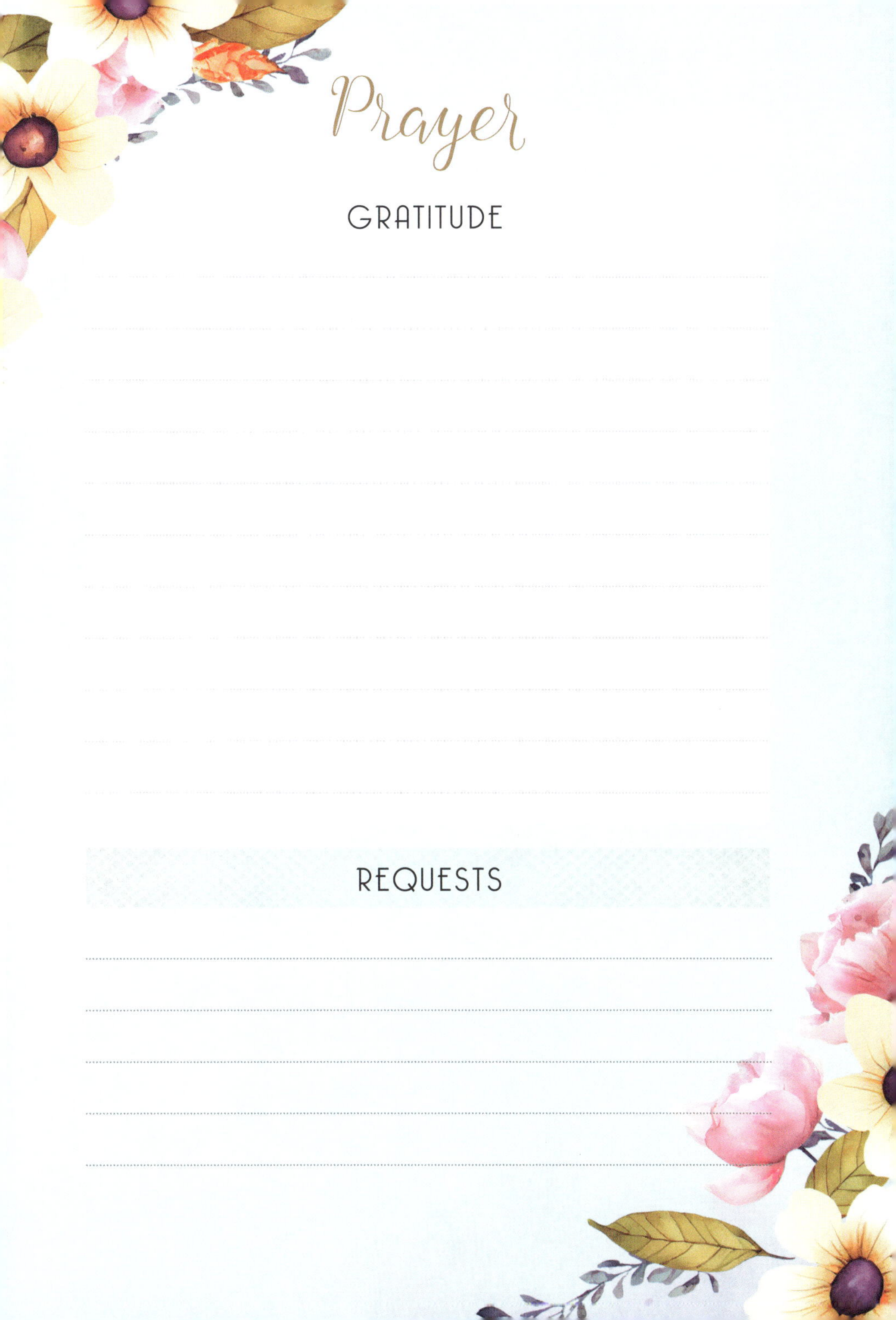

Prayer

GRATITUDE

REQUESTS

WEEK 36

Perfect in Weakness

"My grace is sufficient for you, for My strength is made perfect in weakness." Therefore most gladly I will rather boast in my infirmities, that the power of Christ may rest upon me.

2 CORINTHIANS 12:9 NKJV

Have you ever taken a personality test to identify your strengths and weaknesses? You probably know if you are an introvert or extravert, whether you are creative or administrative, good at speaking, or great at listening. You likely also know all too well what your weaknesses are. You might be over-analytical, self-doubting, unorganized, or lacking empathy. There are areas in our lives that we certainly don't feel proud of.

Paul, on the other hand, says he would rather boast about his weaknesses! Paul knew that his weaknesses made him rely on the power of the Holy Spirit.

You may be facing something that you are worried about because it is outside of your comfort zone. It is not really the weakness in which you boast, but rather the power of Christ that is revealed through your weakness. Will you consider that God can shine through you as you acknowledge your complete reliance on his Holy Spirit?

In what area of your life is God's power most evident?

MY THOUGHTS

MY RESPONSE

I can do all things through Christ, because he gives me strength.

PHILIPPIANS 4:13 NCV

To me, this Scripture feels most like (check one)

☐ A PROMISE ☐ AN INSTRUCTION ☐ A TRUTH

Here's how it impacts me...

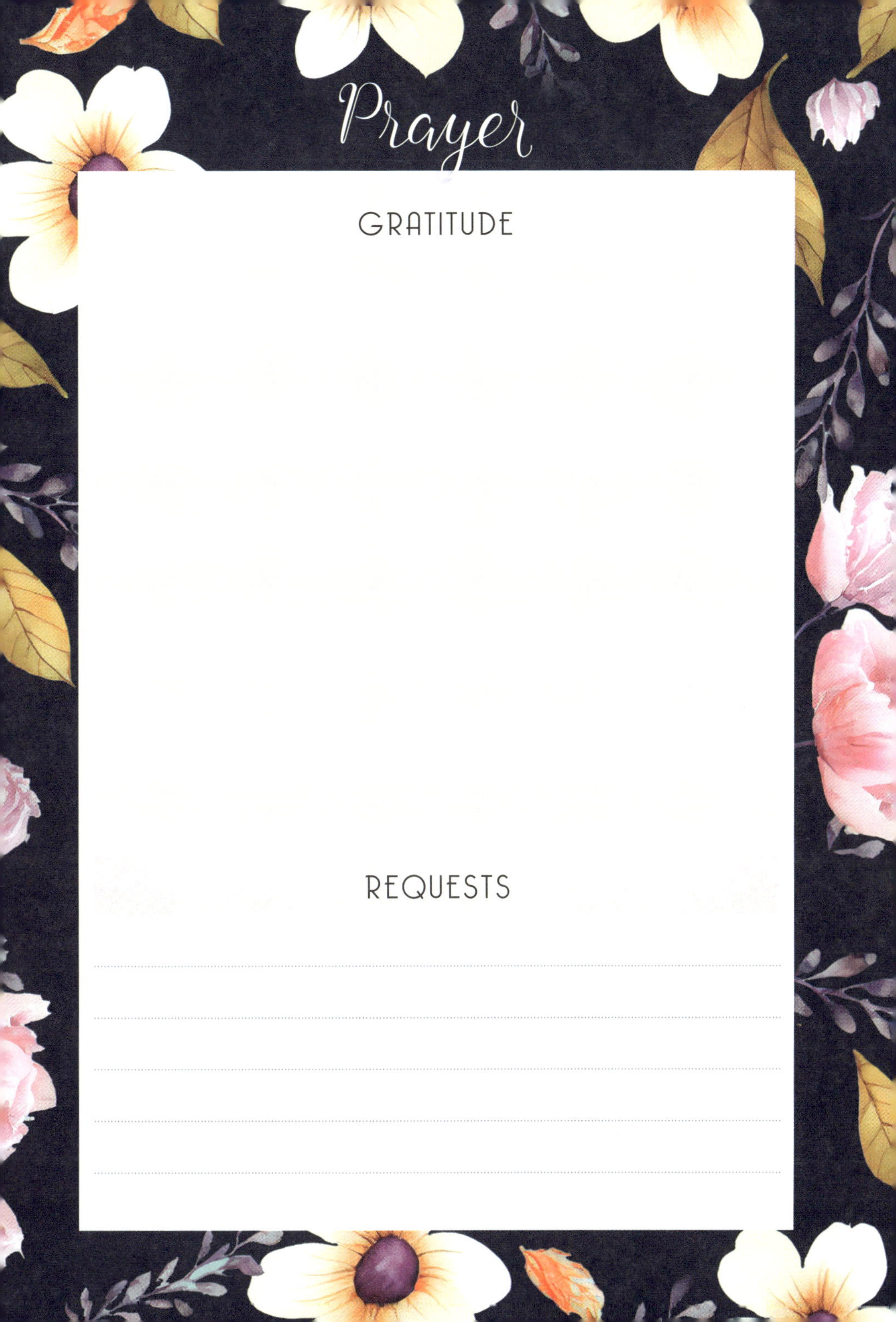
Prayer
GRATITUDE
REQUESTS

WEEK 37

Faulty Comparison

Pay careful attention to your own work, for then you will get the satisfaction of a job well done, and you won't need to compare yourself to anyone else.

GALATIANS 6:4 NLT

In the age of social media, comparison has become an easier default than it's ever been. When every image you see of others has been properly angled, edited, filtered, and cropped, you are quickly led into the delusion that the lives you see portrayed in those images are perfect. You believe that the smiling faces in that post are always smiling, and the perfect homes with beautiful lighting are permanently well-kept and polished.

The danger of these filtered images is that we end up comparing ourselves to something that isn't an accurate standard. What we don't see is the life outside that frame. We don't see the mess, the struggles, and the imperfections that are inevitably part of every life—even the perfect-looking ones.

God wants you to be so invested in the work that he has given you to do that you are not distracted or dissatisfied by what you see someone else doing. Dive headfirst into your own vision, saying yes to contentment and joy and moving forward into greater fulfillment and happiness.

Reflection

What does your unique lifestyle look like? How can you find contentment in it?

MY THOUGHTS

MY RESPONSE

Examine yourselves to see if your faith is genuine. Test yourselves. Surely you know that Jesus Christ is among you; if not, you have failed the test of genuine faith.

2 CORINTHIANS 13:5 NLT

To me, this Scripture feels most like (check one)

☐ A PROMISE ☐ AN INSTRUCTION ☐ A TRUTH

Here's how it impacts me...

....

....

....

....

....

Prayer

GRATITUDE

REQUESTS

WEEK 38

Eternal Fountains

"Whoever drinks the water I give them will never thirst. Indeed, the water I give them will become in them a spring of water welling up to eternal life."

JOHN 4:14 NIV

We take it for granted that when we turn on a faucet, water will come out. If we need something to drink, we can quench our thirst pretty easily. In Jesus' day, people had to get their water from a well that was often situated quite far from their homes. It was a necessary daily task that provided for the family's needs.

Imagine then being offered water that would last forever. This is what Jesus presented to the woman at the well. She would never have to make this trip again in the heat of the day. Jesus compared her desire with a spiritual desire: just as the well was a source for physical life, he was the source for eternal life.

You have received Jesus as the source for your life. Not only does Jesus say that he will provide you with everlasting water, but he says that his water will be like a fountain, springing up. Are you thankful for the eternal life that Jesus has placed within you? Remember to draw from him as your source of life today.

Reflection

What refreshing do you need this week? Are you going to the source of living water for all you need?

MY THOUGHTS

MY RESPONSE

*"Whoever believes in me,
as Scripture has said,
rivers of living water
will flow from within them."*

JOHN 7:38 NIV

To me, this Scripture feels most like (check one)

☐ A PROMISE ☐ AN INSTRUCTION ☐ A TRUTH

Here's how it impacts me...

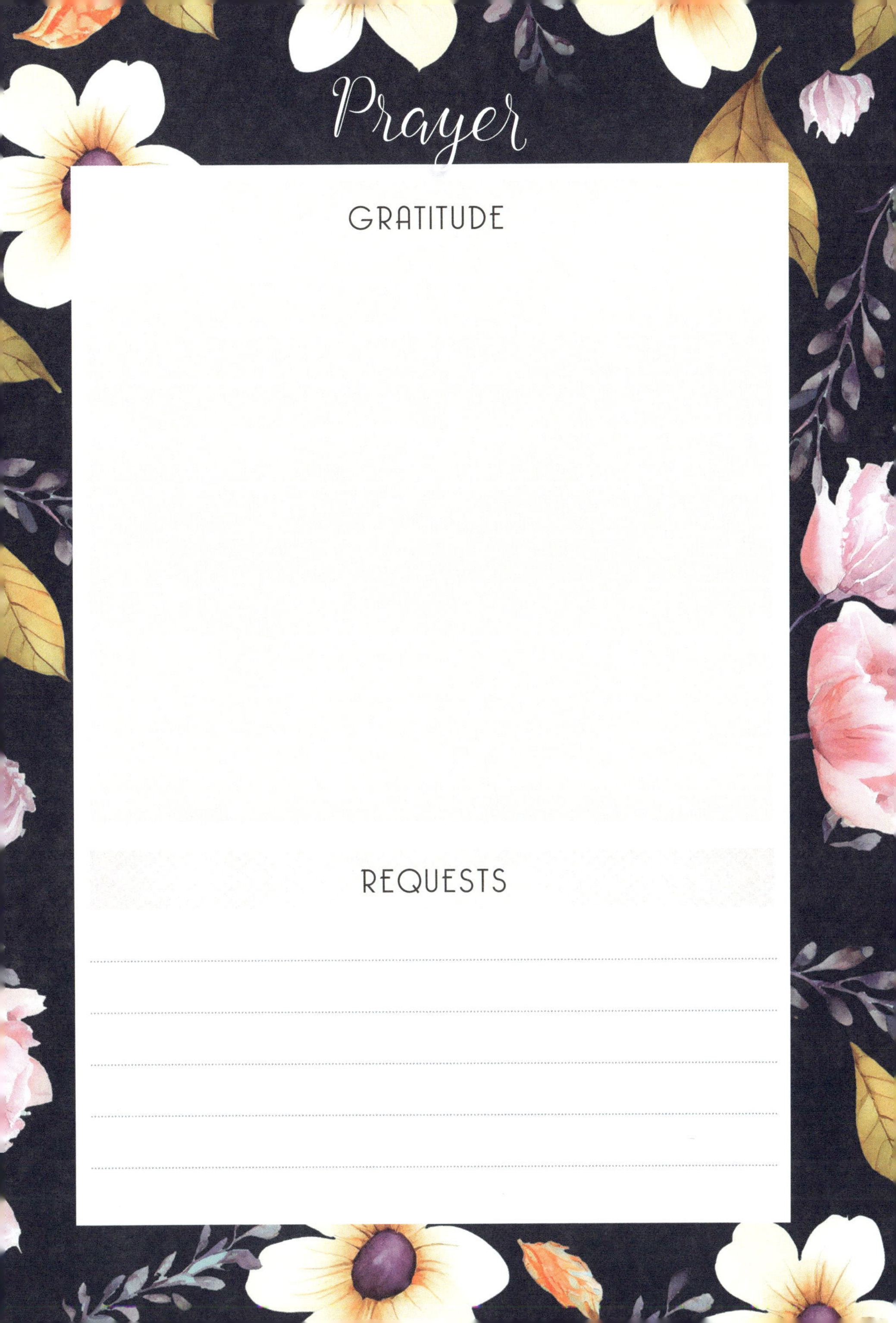

Prayer

GRATITUDE

REQUESTS

WEEK 39

Living Word

> God's word is alive and working and is sharper than a double-edged sword. It cuts all the way into us, where the soul and the spirit are joined, to the center of our joints and bones. And it judges the thoughts and feelings in our hearts.
>
> HEBREWS 4:12 NCV

Have you ever noticed God speaking to you in themes? We all go through different seasons in life, and God speaks to our hearts accordingly. Some of us may be going through a season of learning to wait, while another is learning how to step out in faith. But the beautiful thing about God is that he is big enough to speak to all of us—in our different places, with our different hearts—at the same time, with the same words.

God's Word is alive and active. It can deliver truth to the heart of each person. Two people can get something completely different from the same passage of Scripture because of what God has been doing in each of their hearts separately. Through the body of Christ, we can come together and share what God is teaching us, multiplying our individual growth as we encourage one another.

Never doubt the power of what you hold in your hands when you read the Word of God. Your Creator knows you so intimately because he is the one who handcrafted your soul, and he cares about you enough to speak directly to your heart through his living Word.

Reflection

What has God been speaking to you about lately? How do you find answers in his living Word?

MY THOUGHTS

MY RESPONSE

"Does not my word burn like fire?"
says the LORD.
"Is it not like a mighty hammer
that smashes a rock to pieces?"

JEREMIAH 23:29 NLT

To me, this Scripture feels most like (check one)

☐ A PROMISE ☐ AN INSTRUCTION ☐ A TRUTH

Here's how it impacts me...

....

....

....

....

....

Prayer

GRATITUDE

REQUESTS

"Don't store up for yourselves treasures on earth, where moth and rust destroy and where thieves break in and steal. But store up for yourselves treasures in heaven, where neither moth nor rust destroys, and where thieves don't break in and steal. For where your treasure is, there your heart will be also."

MATTHEW 6:19-21 CSB

Have you ever sat on a beach and watched a child work tirelessly on an elaborate sandcastle? They spend hours perfecting their creation, thoughtfully forming each section, often stepping back to admire their work. But these children are unaware of the patterns of ocean waves and don't realize that as the day passes, their masterpieces will eventually be swept away by the swelling tide. All that work, all that concentration, all that pride gone as the water flattens the sand.

What proverbial castles are we building in our lives that could, at any moment, be flattened? We've got to buy into the bigger vision. We must know what can last and what won't. There are temporary kingdoms and a kingdom that will never pass away.

If your work and your heart are invested in a heavenly vision, then what you have spent your life on will continue to matter for longer than you live.

Reflection

What is your greatest treasure? How is that evident in the way you live?

MY THOUGHTS

MY RESPONSE

Do not wear yourself out to get rich;
do not trust your own cleverness.
Cast but a glance at riches,
and they are gone.

PROVERBS 23:4-5 NIV

To me, this Scripture feels most like (check one)

☐ A PROMISE ☐ AN INSTRUCTION ☐ A TRUTH

Here's how it impacts me...

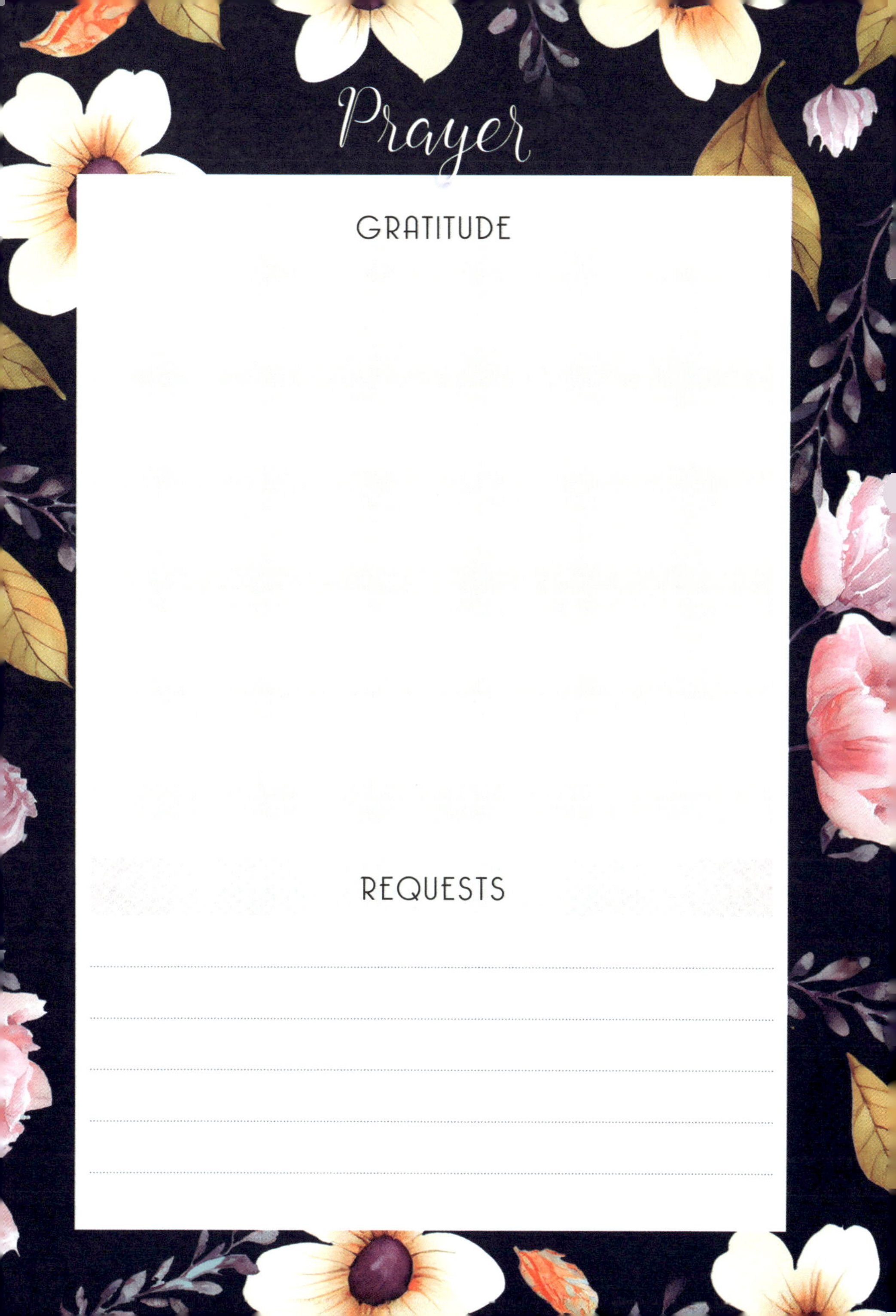

Prayer

GRATITUDE

REQUESTS

WEEK 41

The Spice Rack

> We know that for those who love God all things work together for good, for those who are called according to his purpose.
>
> ROMANS 8:28 ESV

Anyone who does any amount of cooking has a spice rack. There are some spices that get used consistently like garlic, salt, and pepper. And there are other spices that may only be used once in a while like cardamom, tarragon, or anise. While those lesser used spices may collect dust in the back of your spice cupboard, you still rely on them to bring out just the right flavor in that one particular meal.

Life is a lot like a spice rack. We shelve our experiences like spices: some make so much sense, we pull from them often, clearly recognizing their usefulness. Other experiences are more subtle and undeclared; sometimes we go years without understanding why we had them. But then, in one moment, our life recipe will call for a little saffron. And all at once, it will make sense. That experience we had, the one we thought we must've had by mistake, will be the only one that matters for that moment.

Is there a season in your life that you often wonder about? When you can't make sense of why it happened, remember that God will work it *all* for his good because you love him.

Reflection

What experience do you question as being useful? How could you see it as being part of God's purpose to bring about good?

MY THOUGHTS

MY RESPONSE

*In his kindness God called you to share in
his eternal glory by means of Christ Jesus.
So after you have suffered a little while,
he will restore, support, and strengthen you,
and he will place you on a firm foundation.*

1 PETER 5:10 NLT

To me, this Scripture feels most like (check one)

☐ A PROMISE ☐ AN INSTRUCTION ☐ A TRUTH

Here's how it impacts me...

GRATITUDE

REQUESTS

WEEK 42

In the Dark

In him was life, and the life was the light of men. The light shines in the darkness, and the darkness has not overcome it.

JOHN 1:4-5 ESV

Have you ever walked somewhere in the pitch black? You bump into things, knock stuff over, and often can't even place where you are or where you're going. Everything becomes muddled in the darkness. Without light to guide you, you can't see where you're going, or what you're running into.

Many times in the Bible, God likens being in sin to being in darkness. When we immerse ourselves in sin, thus rejecting the light of the truth, we can no longer see what we are running into. The darkness will cloud our thinking and our rationale, and we won't even be able to determine what sins are coming our way. By allowing sinful messages to enter our souls through different avenues, we lose the power to navigate our lives in righteousness.

When wickedness begins to overtake your life, you lose the ability to recognize what is making you sin. Strive to keep your soul sensitive to the truth. Keep sight of the light by spending time in God's Word.

What areas of sin do you easily stumble into? How can you shine light into the darkness in those situations?

MY THOUGHTS

MY RESPONSE

"I am the light of the world. Anyone who follows me will never walk in the darkness but will have the light of life."

JOHN 8:12 CSB

To me, this Scripture feels most like (check one)

☐ A PROMISE ☐ AN INSTRUCTION ☐ A TRUTH

Here's how it impacts me...

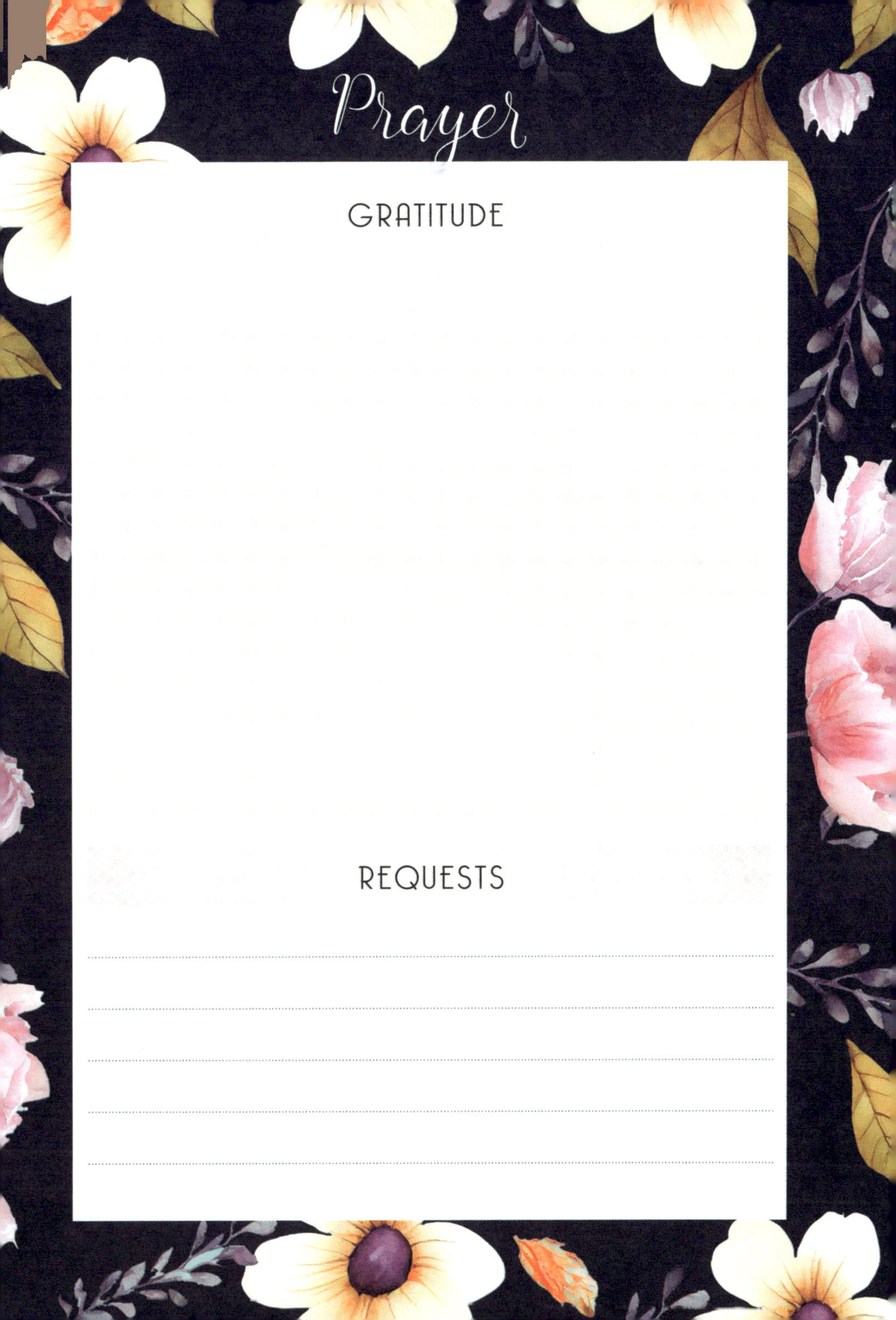

Prayer

GRATITUDE

REQUESTS

WEEK 43

Change of Season

"Be strong and courageous, and do the work. Do not be afraid or discouraged, for the Lord God, my God, is with you. He will not fail you or forsake you."

1 CHRONICLES 28:20 NIV

You will, undoubtedly, have various seasons in your life: seasons of longing and contentment, seasons of discouragement and joy, seasons of more and less. Being an adult means stretching into new ways of living, and this usually doesn't happen until the season hits.

Seasons can be challenging. They require bravery, obedience, dedication, and sometimes total upheaval of everything comfortable in our lives. If we feel that impending corner of a season change in our hearts, it usually means God is preparing us for something different. In those seasons of life, the one who won't change, won't back down, and won't leave us stranded is our heavenly Father.

Do you see an impending season change approaching? How does it make you feel? Be brave! God will not move you into something without giving you the grace you need to make it through.

Reflection

How do you feel about change? Can you submit yourself to God and let him be your strength?

MY THOUGHTS

MY RESPONSE

"Have I not commanded you? Be strong and courageous. Do not be frightened, and do not be dismayed, for the LORD your God is with you wherever you go."

JOSHUA 1:9 ESV

To me, this Scripture feels most like (check one)

☐ A PROMISE ☐ AN INSTRUCTION ☐ A TRUTH

Here's how it impacts me...

Prayer

GRATITUDE

REQUESTS

WEEK 44

Joyous Journey

> When troubles of any kind come your way, consider it an opportunity for great joy. For you know that when your faith is tested, your endurance has a chance to grow. So let it grow, for when your endurance is fully developed, you will be perfect and complete, needing nothing.
>
> JAMES 1:2-4 NLT

There is great joy in the journey: in the mundane details, in the difficult times, in the confusing moments, and in the tears. There is so much joy to be found in the quiet and in the noise.

Pity parties and comparisons create a direct path for the enemy to steal our joy. There is hope in Jesus and the gift of little joy-filled moments. They come in varying forms: sunshine rays pouring in the windows, a nice person at the check-out counter, a turn-the-volume-up kind of song, a dance party in the living room, or the taste of a delicious meal after a long day. Whatever the moment, there is joy if we look for it.

There's a journey of joy in waking up every day knowing it's another day to breathe in the fresh air, head to dinner with a friend, or grab coffee with a co-worker. Find joy in the moment.

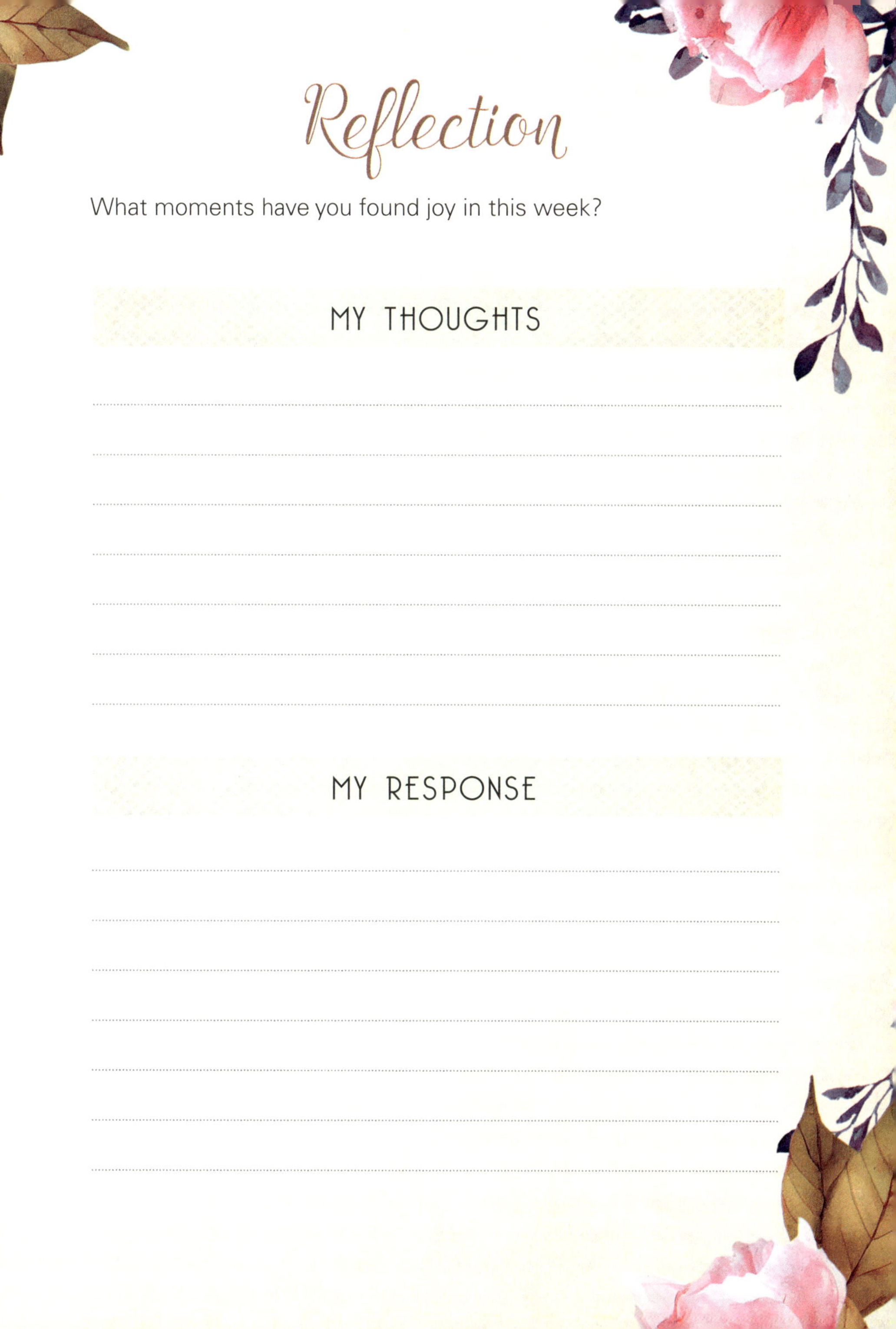

Reflection

What moments have you found joy in this week?

MY THOUGHTS

MY RESPONSE

Blessed is the one who endures trials, because when he has stood the test he will receive the crown of life that God has promised to those who love him.

JAMES 1:12 CSB

To me, this Scripture feels most like (check one)

☐ A PROMISE ☐ AN INSTRUCTION ☐ A TRUTH

Here's how it impacts me...

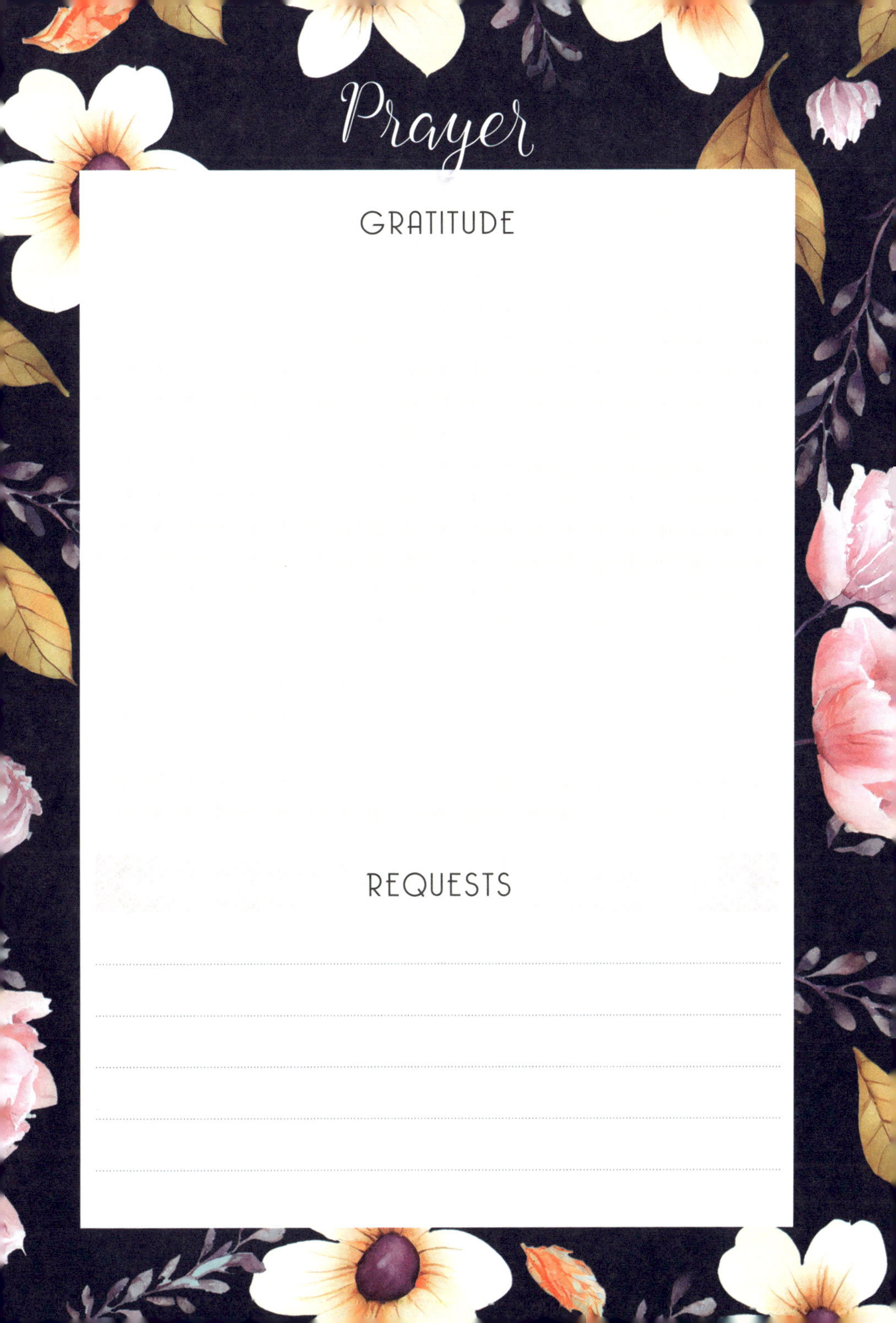

Prayer

GRATITUDE

REQUESTS

WEEK 45

He Knows

> The Holy Spirit helps us in our weakness. For example, we don't know what God wants us to pray for. But the Holy Spirit prays for us with groanings that cannot be expressed in words.
>
> ROMANS 8:26 NLT

You stare at the menu, overwhelmed by choices. Pasta sounds yummy, but you're avoiding carbs. Salad sounds healthy, but you just had that for lunch. Steak sounds perfect until you look at the price. Everyone else has ordered: all eyes are on you. You know you're hungry, you just don't know what for. "What do I want?" you ask, though not expecting an answer.

There are days prayer can feel like that. We know we want something, we sense an ache or longing, but can't quite identify it. Other times, we're simply in too much pain to focus. We need, we need... but we can't get the words out. "What do I want?" we cry. This time, we *can* expect an answer.

The Holy Spirit, because he lives inside us, knows us so intimately he can actually step in and pray on our behalf. He knows even when we don't. Spend some time with the Spirit today. Thank him for knowing your heart and sharing it with God when you can't.

Are you overwhelmed by choices? How can you let the Holy Spirit pray for you this week?

MY THOUGHTS

MY RESPONSE

"It is not you who speak,
but the Spirit of your Father
speaking through you."

MATTHEW 10:20 ESV

To me, this Scripture feels most like (check one)

☐ A PROMISE ☐ AN INSTRUCTION ☐ A TRUTH

Here's how it impacts me...

Prayer

GRATITUDE

REQUESTS

WEEK 46

Being Known

> You know what I long for, Lord;
> you hear my every sigh.
>
> PSALM 38:9 NLT

Think of the most perfect gift you've ever received. Not the most extravagant, but the one that was just so perfectly *you* that you realized the giver really knew you. They heard you, that one time, when you mentioned that one thing, perhaps in passing, and because they were listening with their heart, they saw into yours. They get you.

We love to be understood, and long to be seen. For many of us it's how we know we are loved. How much, then, must the Father love us? He who knows everything about us, who takes the time to listen to every longing and comfort every sigh, is waiting to give us his perfect gifts. We are known. We are loved.

Share your longing with God today. Let him show you his great love by revealing how intimately he knows you. Let him give you a good and perfect gift.

Reflection

What are you asking your good Father for this week?

MY THOUGHTS

MY RESPONSE

*LORD, you have heard the desire of the humble;
you will strengthen their hearts.
You will listen carefully.*

PSALM 10:17 CSB

To me, this Scripture feels most like (check one)

☐ A PROMISE ☐ AN INSTRUCTION ☐ A TRUTH

Here's how it impacts me...

Prayer

GRATITUDE

REQUESTS

WEEK 47

Remain Seated

"Remain in me, as I also remain in you. No branch can bear fruit by itself; it must remain in the vine. Neither can you bear fruit unless you remain in me."

JOHN 15:4 NIV

When riding in a moving car, boat, or plane, we wouldn't just jump out, no matter how restless or impatient we were feeling. That would be crazy. We couldn't possibly expect to arrive at our destination as safely or as quickly—or perhaps at all. We grasp the necessity of remaining where we are if we want to get where we intended to go.

Why are we so quick to jump ahead when it comes to God's plans for our lives? We accept his grace but not his timing. We welcome his comfort but not his discipline. How often do we decide without praying, or act without his prompting? And yet we expect to get where we are going—safely, quickly, easily.

Are there areas of your life you are trying to direct on your own? Spend some time praying for the Spirit to reveal to you where you are not abiding in Jesus or trusting his timing. Ask him to help you trust him.

Reflection

Where might you need to remain seated this week?

MY THOUGHTS

MY RESPONSE

Anyone who runs ahead and does not continue in the teaching of Christ does not have God; whoever continues in the teaching has both the Father and the Son.

2 JOHN 1:9 NIV

To me, this Scripture feels most like (check one)

☐ A PROMISE ☐ AN INSTRUCTION ☐ A TRUTH

Here's how it impacts me...

....

....

....

....

....

Prayer

GRATITUDE

REQUESTS

WEEK 48

Where Credit Is Due

"Give praise to the LORD, proclaim his name;
make known among the nations what he has done,
and proclaim that his name is exalted.
Sing to the LORD, for he has done glorious things;
let this be known to all the world."

ISAIAH 12:4-5 NIV

You achieve a goal, or you get some wonderful news. The day you've been waiting for has arrived, and you're so excited about it. What is your first reaction? Do you update your status on social media to let your friends know what you've done? Do you call your mom and tell her the wonderful news?

There's nothing wrong with sharing your excitement with others. But when doing so, be sure to give the glory and praise to God. He has given you everything you have. Get excited about how good he has been to you. When you're so happy that you can't help but dance for joy, be sure to give Jesus a twirl too. He wants to celebrate with you!

Are you giving credit where it's due? Be sure to take some time today to thank the Lord for all that he has helped you achieve and for all that he has given you. He wants to share in your excitement!

What are you excited about right now? How can you share that excitement with God?

MY THOUGHTS

MY RESPONSE

Oh give thanks to the LORD;
call upon his name;
make known his deeds
among the peoples!

PSALM 105:1 ESV

To me, this Scripture feels most like (check one)

☐ A PROMISE ☐ AN INSTRUCTION ☐ A TRUTH

Here's how it impacts me...

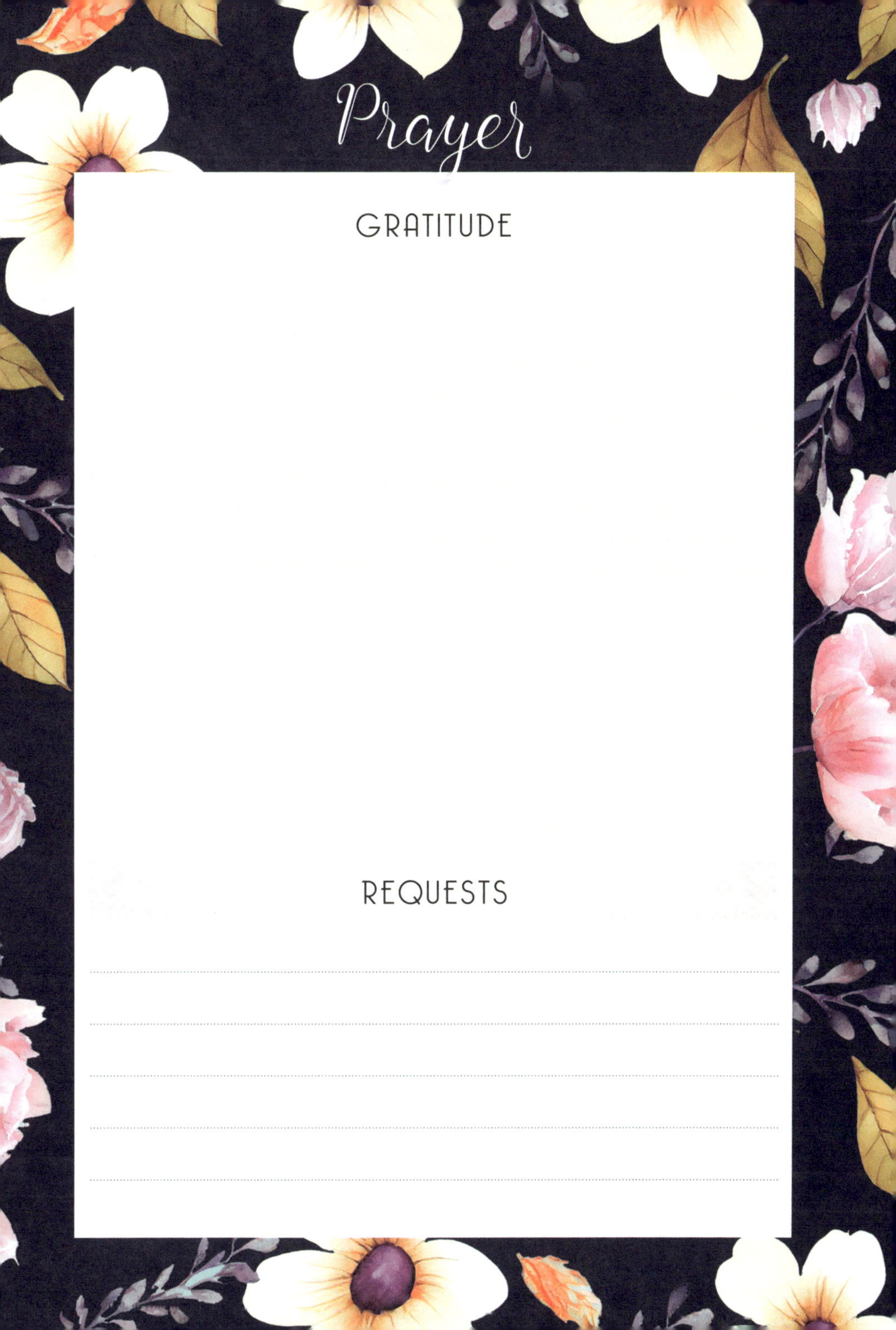

Prayer

GRATITUDE

REQUESTS

WEEK 49

Weary to the Core

> A person's steps are established by the LORD,
> and he takes pleasure in his way.
> Though he falls, he will not be overwhelmed,
> because the LORD supports him with his hand.
>
> PSALM 37:23-24 CSB

Have you ever been run so ragged that you just didn't know if you could take even one more step? Your calendar is a blur of scheduled activities, your days are full, your every hour is blocked off for this or that, and it's hard to find even a spare minute for yourself. Your very bones feel weary, and you fall into bed at night, drained from it all.

There is someone who is ready to catch you when you fall. You might stumble throughout your busy day, but he will never let you hit the floor as you take a tumble. God delights in you! He will direct your every step if you ask him to. He will gladly take you by the hand and guide you.

Though you may be weary, God has enough energy to get you through anything. Take his hand today and let him lead you.

Reflection

How can you allow God to guide your days and lead you out of your weariness?

MY THOUGHTS

MY RESPONSE

The LORD upholds all who are falling
and raises up all who are bowed down.

PSALM 145:14 ESV

To me, this Scripture feels most like (check one)

☐ A PROMISE ☐ AN INSTRUCTION ☐ A TRUTH

Here's how it impacts me...

Prayer

GRATITUDE

REQUESTS

WEEK 50

Losing to Gain

"Whoever wants to save their life will lose it, but whoever loses his life for me will find it."

MATTHEW 16:25 NIV

The key to growing in our faith is simple. There must be less of *us* in order to have more of God. To allow more of his presence into our lives, we must give up more of ourselves. We need to place our lives before him as an offering and give him our all.

The world would say that giving up ourselves is a loss. We've been taught that we must put ourselves first. We need to make ourselves a priority. But that is truly missing out! When we give ourselves over completely to God, we get to share in his glory and in his great joy. Setting aside our earthly pleasures for heavenly treasures means we gain a lot more than what this world could ever offer us.

What desires do you find yourself holding onto? Empty yourself of the desires of your flesh and allow God to fill you with his presence. You won't feel a lack. In fact, it will overflow in your life, spilling out everywhere for others to see.

Reflection

What does it look like for you to lose your life in Christ?

MY THOUGHTS

MY RESPONSE

"Those who love their lives will lose them,
but those who hate their lives in this world
will keep true life forever."

JOHN 12:25 NCV

To me, this Scripture feels most like (check one)

☐ A PROMISE ☐ AN INSTRUCTION ☐ A TRUTH

Here's how it impacts me...

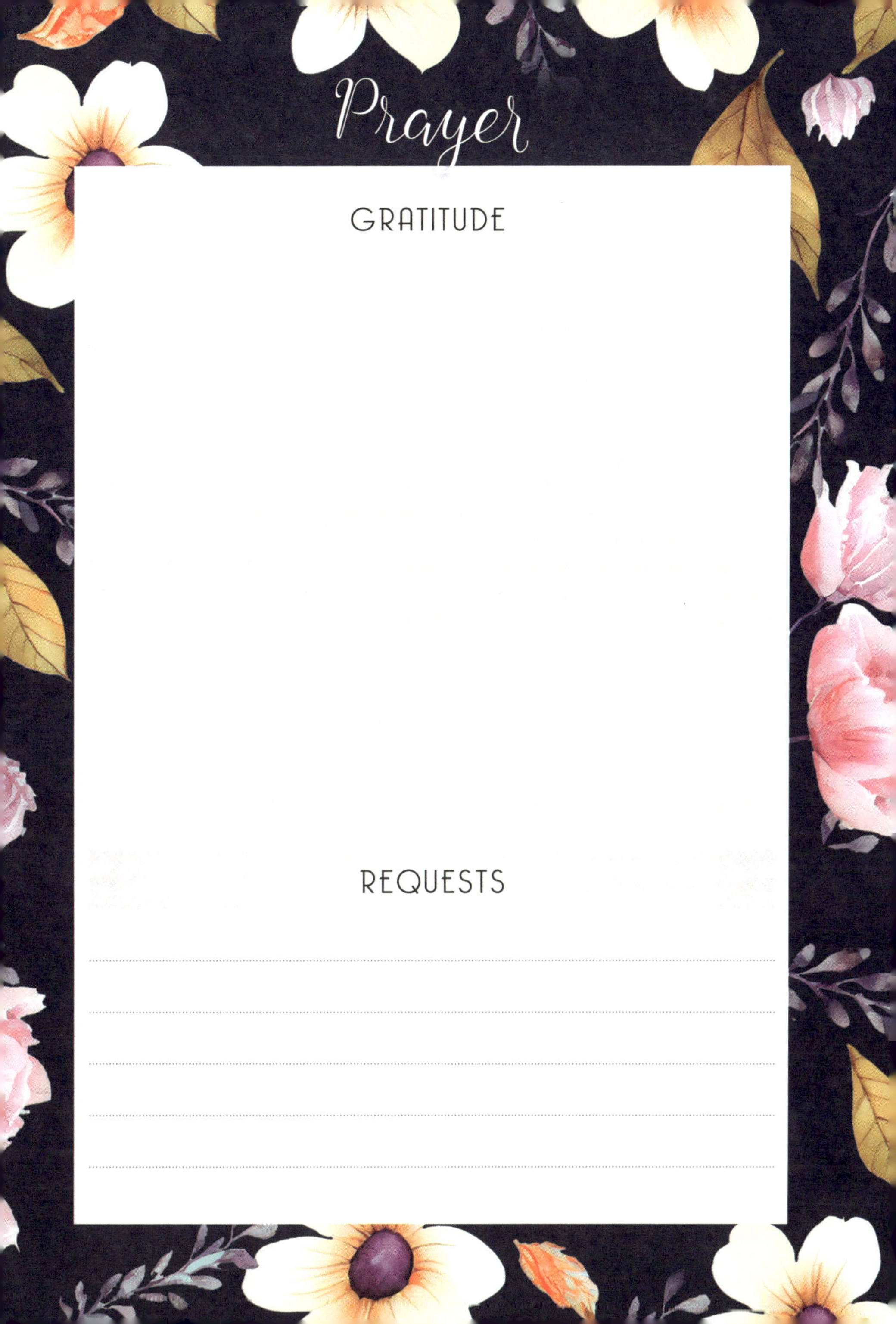

Prayer

GRATITUDE

REQUESTS

WEEK 51

You Have Time

> Pay careful attention, then, to how you walk—not as unwise people but as wise—making the most of the time, because the days are evil. So don't be foolish, but understand what the Lord's will is.
>
> EPHESIANS 5:15-17 CSB

Time is one of those things we never seem to have enough of. Many of our days feel like a race against the clock. We seem to lack the time we need for even the most important things: things like being in God's Word, spending intentional time with loved ones, or volunteering to help those in need.

At the end of the day, there is one reality we must remember: we have time for what we make time for. It's easy to feel busy, but what are we truly busying ourselves with? Are we finding time to spend browsing social media or watching re-runs of our favorite TV shows? Are we finding time to take a long shower or sleep for a few extra minutes in the morning? None of those things are necessarily *wrong,* but if we feel pressed for time and are unable to spend time with God, we may need to rethink where our time goes.

Take a good hard look at your day today. Spend your time in a way that will make the most of the moments and opportunities you have.

Reflection

How will you choose to spend your time this week? Is there something you can move to make time for important things?

MY THOUGHTS

MY RESPONSE

Live wisely among those
who are not believers,
and make the most
of every opportunity.

COLOSSIANS 4:5 NLT

To me, this Scripture feels most like (check one)

☐ A PROMISE ☐ AN INSTRUCTION ☐ A TRUTH

Here's how it impacts me...

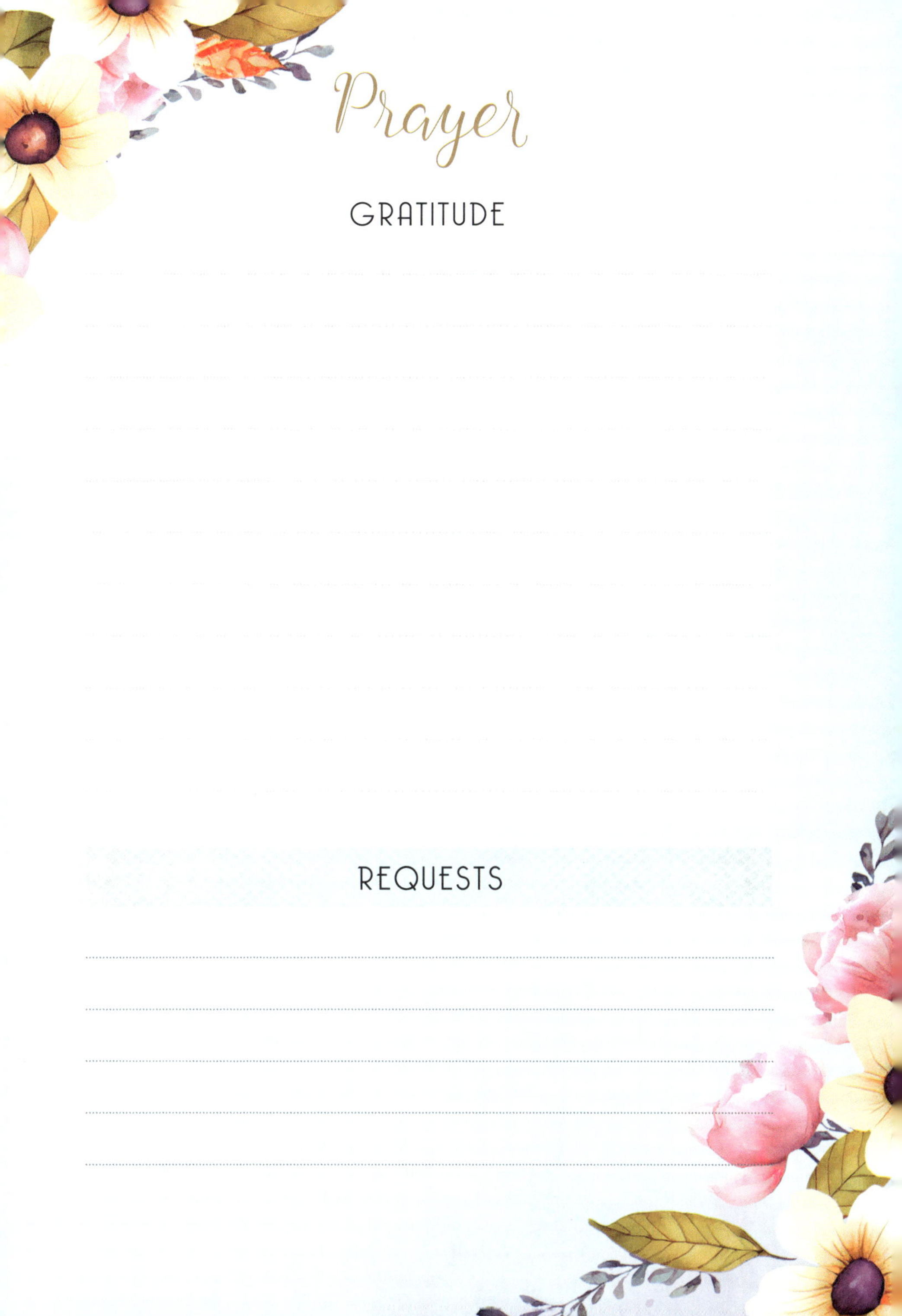

Prayer

GRATITUDE

REQUESTS

WEEK 52

Thirsty for More

I long, yes I faint with longing
to enter the courts of the LORD.
With my whole being, body and soul,
I will shout joyfully to the living God.

PSALM 84:2 NLT

Have you ever noticed that the more consistently you drink water, the more your body thirsts for it? And the less you drink water, the less you consciously desire it. Though you still need water to live, you become satisfied with small amounts of it disguised in other foods and drinks. But for a body that has become accustomed to pure water on a daily basis, only straight water will quench its thirst.

The same principle applies to God's presence in our lives. The more we enter his presence, the more we long to stay there. The more we sit at his feet and listen to what he has to say, the more we need his Word to guide us. But if we allow ourselves to become satisfied with candy-coated truth and secondhand revelation, we will slowly begin to lose our hunger for the pure, untainted presence of the living God.

Press into Jesus until you can no longer be satisfied with anything less than the purest form of his presence. Cultivate your hunger and your fascination with him until you crave him. Spend your life feasting on his truth, knowing his character, and adoring his heart.

Does your entire being long to be with God? How can you create this longing in your heart?

MY THOUGHTS

MY RESPONSE

As the deer pants for streams of water,
so my soul pants for you, my God.
My soul thirsts for God, for the living God.
When can I go and meet with God?

PSALM 42:1-2 NIV

To me, this Scripture feels most like (check one)

☐ A PROMISE ☐ AN INSTRUCTION ☐ A TRUTH

Here's how it impacts me...

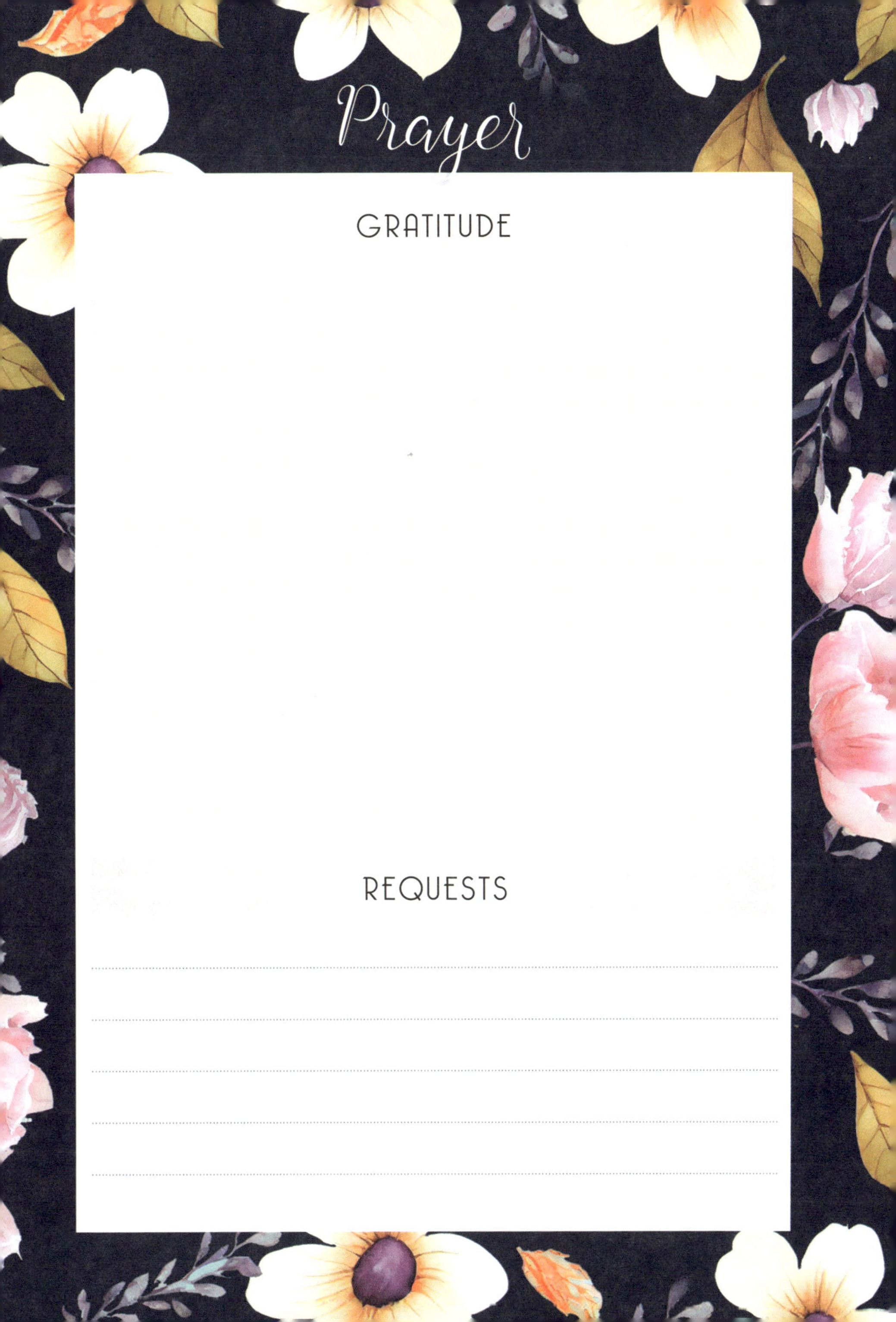
Prayer
GRATITUDE
REQUESTS

Notes

Notes

Notes

Notes

Notes

Notes

Notes

Notes

Notes

Notes

Notes